NO FEAR SHAKESPEARE

NO FEAR SHAKESPEARE

Antony and Cleopatra
As You Like It
The Comedy of Errors
Coriolanus
Hamlet
Henry IV, Parts One and Two
Henry V
Julius Caesar
King Lear
Macbeth
Measure for Measure
The Merchant of Venice
A Midsummer Night's Dream
Much Ado About Nothing
Othello
Richard II
Richard III
Romeo and Juliet
Sonnets
The Taming of the Shrew
The Tempest
Twelfth Night
Winter's Tale

NO FEAR SHAKESPEARE

TWO GENTLEMEN OF VERONA

*sparknotes

SPARKNOTES and NO FEAR SHAKESPEARE
are registered trademarks of SparkNotes LLC.

Text © 2017 Sterling Publishing Co., Inc.
Cover © 2017 Sterling Publishing Co., Inc.

All rights reserved. No part of this publication may be reproduced,
stored in a retrieval system, or transmitted in any form or by any
means (including electronic, mechanical, photocopying, recording, or
otherwise) without prior written permission from the publisher.

ISBN 978-1-4549-2807-2

Distributed in Canada by Sterling Publishing Co., Inc.
c/o Canadian Manda Group, 664 Annette Street
Toronto, Ontario M6S 2C8, Canada
Distributed in the United Kingdom by GMC Distribution Services
Castle Place, 166 High Street, Lewes, East Sussex BN7 1XU, England
Distributed in Australia by NewSouth Books
45 Beach Street, Coogee, NSW 2034, Australia

For information about custom editions, special sales, and premium
and corporate purchases, please contact Sterling Special Sales at
800-805-5489 or specialsales@sterlingpublishing.com.

Manufactured in the United States of America

Lot #:
2 4 6 8 10 9 7 5 3 1

10/17

sterlingpublishing.com
sparknotes.com

Cover and title page illustration by Richard Amari.

There's matter in these sighs, these profound heaves.
You must translate: 'tis fit we understand them.
(*Hamlet,* 4.1.1–2)

FEAR NOT.

Have you ever found yourself looking at a Shakespeare play, then down at the footnotes, then back up at the play, and still not understanding? You know what the individual words mean, but they don't add up. SparkNotes' *No Fear Shakespeare* will help you break through all that. Put the pieces together with our easy-to-read translations. Soon you'll be reading Shakespeare's own words fearlessly—and actually enjoying it.

No Fear Shakespeare puts Shakespeare's language side-by-side with a facing-page translation into modern English—the kind of English people actually speak today. When Shakespeare's words make your head spin, our translation will help you sort out what's happening, who's saying what, and why.

TWO GENTLEMEN OF VERONA

Characters ix

ACT ONE
Scene 1 2
Scene 2 16
Scene 3 30

ACT TWO
Scene 1 38
Scene 2 54
Scene 3 58
Scene 4 64
Scene 5 84
Scene 6 90
Scene 7 94

ACT THREE
Scene 1 102
Scene 2 132

ACT FOUR
Scene 1 140
Scene 2 148
Scene 3 162
Scene 4 166

ACT FIVE
Scene 1 182
Scene 2 184
Scene 3 190
Scene 4 192

CHARACTERS

Proteus—Valentine's supposed best friend and one of the titular gentlemen of Verona. Proteus is Julia's sweetheart at the beginning of the play, but when he joins Valentine at the duke's palace, he falls in love with Silvia and attempts to steal her away from Valentine.

Valentine—Proteus's best friend and Silvia's love. Valentine is the other titular gentleman of Verona. Banished to the forest after Proteus betrays to the duke Valentine's plan to elope with Silvia, he becomes king of the outlaws.

Julia—Proteus's beloved, Julia, is mistress of the servant Lucetta. Julia disguises herself as Sebastian, an aristocratic male page, when she travels to Milan to visit Proteus. As the page, she does Proteus's bidding, delivering to his new beloved, Silvia, the very ring she herself had earlier given him as a gift.

Silvia—The duke's daughter and beloved of Valentine. Proteus and Thurio also vie for her affections. Silvia commiserates with Sebastian over the wrong that Proteus has done to Julia. She escapes her father's palace with the help of Sir Eglamour, who abandons her at the sight of the outlaws.

Duke of Milan—Silvia's father. He wants Silvia to marry the boorish but wealthy suitor Thurio. Upon hearing of Valentine's plot to elope with Silvia, the duke banishes Valentine.

Lucetta—Julia's servant. She considers love from a practical point of view and helps Julia disguise herself as a man.

Launce—Proteus' servant and the master of a poorly trained mutt named Crab. His devotion to his dog knows no bounds and gives the play much humor. Launce falls in love with an unattractive but wealthy maid.

Speed—Valentine's page. At the beginning of the play, Speed does Proteus's bidding as well. He is friendly with Launce.

Thurio—A foolish rival to Valentine for Silvia's hand. Thurio is wealthy and unpleasant.

Sir Eglamour—The gentleman Silvia calls upon to help her escape from the duke's court.

Antonio—Proteus's father and the master of the servant Panthino.

Host—The person who houses Julia while she searches for Proteus.

Outlaws—A crew of bandits who make Valentine their king when he is banished.

Crab—Launce's dog.

Panthino—Antonio's servant.

NO FEAR SHAKESPEARE

TWO GENTLEMEN OF VERONA

ACT ONE
SCENE 1

Enter VALENTINE *and* PROTEUS

VALENTINE
    Cease to persuade, my loving Proteus;
    Home-keeping youth have ever homely wits.
    Were't not affection chains thy tender days
    To the sweet glances of thy honored love,
5   I rather would entreat thy company
    To see the wonders of the world abroad
    Than, living dully sluggardized at home,
    Wear out thy youth with shapeless idleness.
    But since thou lov'st, love still and thrive therein,
10   Even as I would when I to love begin.

PROTEUS
    Wilt thou be gone? Sweet Valentine, adieu!
    Think on thy Proteus when thou haply seest
    Some rare noteworthy object in thy travel.
    Wish me partaker in thy happiness
15   When thou dost meet good hap; and in thy danger,
    If ever danger do environ thee,
    Commend thy grievance to my holy prayers,
    For I will be thy beadsman, Valentine.

VALENTINE
    And on a love book pray for my success?

PROTEUS
20   Upon some book I love I'll pray for thee.

VALENTINE
    That's on some shallow story of deep love,
    How young Leander crossed the Hellespont.

ACT ONE
SCENE 1

VALENTINE *and* **PROTEUS** *enter.*

St. Valentine is the patron saint of lovers.

VALENTINE

Stop trying to persuade me, **Proteus**. Young homebodies have dull minds. If you weren't so tied to the girl you love, I'd ask you to come with me to see the distant wonders of the world rather than waste your youth living aimlessly as a sluggard at home. But, since you're in love, keep on loving and thrive in your love. I would do the same were I in love.

In Greek mythology, Proteus was a sea god who could change shape. The name suggests that Shakespeare's Proteus frequently changes his mind.

PROTEUS

Are you going now? Goodbye, Valentine, my dear friend! Think of me when you happen to see some rare and noteworthy object in your travels. Wish me happiness, too, when you have good fortune. And if you're ever in danger, trust that my prayers will protect you, for I will pray for you, Valentine.

Valentine implies that Proteus makes love, as opposed to the Bible, his religion.

VALENTINE

And you'll be praying for me on **a book about love**, I suspect?

PROTEUS

I'll pray for you on a book I love.

VALENTINE

No doubt on some shallow story of "true" love, like the one about young **Leander crossing the Hellespont.**

In classical mythology, Leander swam across the Hellespont each night to see his love, Hero. But he drowned in a storm during his crossing one night.

PROTEUS
>That's a deep story of a deeper love,
>For he was more than over shoes in love.

VALENTINE
>'Tis true; for you are over boots in love,
>And yet you never swam the Hellespont.

PROTEUS
>Over the boots? Nay, give me not the boots.

VALENTINE
>No, I will not, for it boots thee not.

PROTEUS
>What?

VALENTINE
>To be in love, where scorn is bought with groans,
>Coy looks with heartsore sighs, one fading moment's mirth
>With twenty watchful, weary, tedious nights.
>If haply won, perhaps a hapless gain;
>If lost, why then a grievous labour won;
>However, but a folly bought with wit,
>Or else a wit by folly vanquishèd.

PROTEUS
>So, by your circumstance, you call me fool.

VALENTINE
>So, by your circumstance, I fear you'll prove.

PROTEUS
>'Tis love you cavil at. I am not Love.

VALENTINE
>Love is your master, for he masters you;
>And he that is so yoked by a fool
>Methinks, should not be chronicled for wise.

PROTEUS
>Yet writers say, as in the sweetest bud
>The eating canker dwells, so eating love
>Inhabits in the finest wits of all.

ACT 1, SCENE 1
NO FEAR SHAKESPEARE

PROTEUS
> That's a deep story of a deeper love—the love was so deep it covered his shoes.

VALENTINE
> It's true. And your love is so deep it covers your boots, and yet you never swam across the Hellespont.

PROTEUS
> Covers my boots? Don't make fun of me.

VALENTINE
> No, I won't, for it doesn't benefit you any.

PROTEUS
> What?

VALENTINE
> When you're in love, your lovesick groans only earn her scorn, your brokenhearted sighs just get you flirtatious glances, and twenty tedious, sleepless nights spent pining for your sweetheart only yield you a brief moment of happiness. If by chance you succeed, it may turn out to be an unlucky win. And if you don't, then you've only managed to waste your time. Either way, you win foolishness by being clever, or your cleverness is killed by foolishness.

PROTEUS
> So, by your logic, I'm a fool.

VALENTINE
> Because of your logic, I fear you'll become a fool.

PROTEUS
> It's love you have a problem with. But don't blame me—I'm not Love.

VALENTINE
> Love is your master, because he's got the better of you. And in my opinion, anyone who's been taken in by a fool shouldn't be considered very wise himself.

PROTEUS
> Yet writers say that just as the destructive caterpillar dwells within the sweetest flower buds, love inhabits the cleverest minds.

MODERN TEXT

VALENTINE
    And writers say, as the most forward bud
    Is eaten by the canker ere it blow,
    Even so by love the young and tender wit
50   Is turned to folly, blasting in the bud,
    Losing his verdure even in the prime,
    And all the fair effects of future hopes.
    But wherefore waste I time to counsel thee
    That art a votary to fond desire?
55   Once more adieu! My father at the road
    Expects my coming, there to see me shipped.

PROTEUS
    And thither will I bring thee, Valentine.

VALENTINE
    Sweet Proteus, no. Now let us take our leave.
    To Milan let me hear from thee by letters
60   Of thy success in love, and what news else
    Betideth here in absence of thy friend;
    And I likewise will visit thee with mine.

PROTEUS
    All happiness bechance to thee in Milan!

VALENTINE
    As much to you at home! And so, farewell!

Exit **VALENTINE**

PROTEUS
65   He after honor hunts, I after love.
    He leaves his friends to dignify them more;
    I leave myself, my friends, and all, for love.
    Thou, Julia, thou hast metamorphosed me,
    Made me neglect my studies, lose my time,
70   War with good counsel, set the world at naught;
    Made wit with musing weak, heart sick with thought.

Enter **SPEED**

ACT 1, SCENE 1
NO FEAR SHAKESPEARE

VALENTINE
> And writers also say that just as the caterpillar eats the greatest flower bud before it blooms, so too does love make young and fragile minds foolish. It destroys the young lover, who loses his youth while still in his prime, and takes away all his future hopes. But why am I wasting my time giving advice to you, a man who is devoted to foolish love? So, once again, farewell! My father expects to meet me at the harbor to see my ship off.

PROTEUS
> I'll go with you, Valentine.

VALENTINE
> My dear Proteus, no. We should say good-bye to each other now. Write to me in Milan, and tell me of your luck with love and whatever other news happens while I'm away. I'll likewise write to you.

PROTEUS
> May you find happiness in Milan!

VALENTINE
> And the same to you here at home! Farewell!

VALENTINE exits.

PROTEUS
> He hunts for honor, while I hunt for love. He leaves his friends to bring them more honor, but I neglect myself, my friends, and everything else for love. Oh, Julia, you've transformed me. You've made me neglect my studies, waste my time, argue against all reasonable advice, and set myself against the world. You've made my brain weak from thinking about you so much, and my heart sick with melancholy.

SPEED enters.

MODERN TEXT

SPEED
Sir Proteus, save you! Saw you my master?

PROTEUS
But now he parted hence, to embark for Milan.

SPEED
Twenty to one, then, he is shipped already,
And I have played the sheep in losing him.

PROTEUS
Indeed, a sheep doth very often stray,
An if the shepherd be a while away.

SPEED
You conclude that my master is a shepherd, then, and I a sheep?

PROTEUS
I do.

SPEED
Why then, my horns are his horns, whether I wake or sleep.

PROTEUS
A silly answer, and fitting well a sheep.

SPEED
This proves me still a sheep.

PROTEUS
True; and thy master a shepherd.

SPEED
Nay, that I can deny by a circumstance.

PROTEUS
It shall go hard, but I'll prove it by another.

SPEED
The shepherd seeks the sheep, and not the sheep the shepherd; but I seek my master, and my master seeks not me. Therefore I am no sheep.

PROTEUS
The sheep for fodder follow the shepherd; the shepherd for food follows not the sheep. Thou for wages followest thy master; thy master for wages follows not thee. Therefore thou art a sheep.

ACT 1, SCENE 1
NO FEAR SHAKESPEARE

SPEED
God save you, Sir Proteus! Have you seen my master?

PROTEUS
He just left here a minute ago on his way to Milan.

SPEED
I'd wager twenty to one, then, that his ship has already left. I'm foolish for having lost him.

PROTEUS
Indeed, sheep often go astray when the shepherd has gone away.

SPEED
You're saying that my master is a shepherd, then, and I'm a sheep?

PROTEUS
Yes.

SPEED
Well then, my horns are his horns, whether I'm awake or asleep.

PROTEUS
What a silly answer—very fitting for a sheep.

SPEED
This means you think I'm still a sheep.

PROTEUS
Yes, and your master a shepherd.

SPEED
No, I can disprove that with an example.

PROTEUS
It'll be a challenge, but I'll prove it with another example.

SPEED
The shepherd looks for the sheep, but the sheep doesn't look for the shepherd. I'm looking for my master, but my master isn't looking for me. Therefore, I'm not a sheep.

PROTEUS
The sheep follows the shepherd because it wants food, but the shepherd doesn't follow the sheep for food. You follow your master for your pay, but your master doesn't follow you for pay. Therefore, you're a sheep.

MODERN TEXT

SPEED
Such another proof will make me cry "Baa."
PROTEUS
But dost thou hear? Gavest thou my letter to Julia?

SPEED
Ay, sir. I, a lost mutton, gave your letter to her, a laced mutton, and she, a laced mutton, gave me, a lost mutton, nothing for my labor.
PROTEUS
Here's too small a pasture for such store of muttons.
SPEED
If the ground be overcharged, you were best stick her.
PROTEUS
Nay, in that you are astray: 'twere best pound you.
SPEED
Nay, sir, less than a pound shall serve me for carrying your letter.
PROTEUS
You mistake. I mean the pound—a pinfold.

SPEED
From a pound to a pin? Fold it over and over,
'Tis threefold too little for carrying a letter to your lover.

PROTEUS
But what said she?
SPEED
(*Nodding*) Ay.
PROTEUS
Nod-ay—why, that's "noddy."
SPEED
You mistook, sir. I say she did nod, and you ask me if she did nod, and I say, "Ay."
PROTEUS
And that set together is "noddy."

ACT 1, SCENE 1
NO FEAR SHAKESPEARE

SPEED
> Another bad example like that and I'll say, "Baa."

PROTEUS
> But anyway, what happened? Did you give my letter to Julia?

SPEED
> Yes, sir. I, a lost mutton, gave your letter to her, a **laced mutton**. And she, the prostitute, gave me, a lost mutton, nothing for all my hard work.

A mutton is a full grown sheep. The term mutton *used in Shakespeare's original was slang for prostitute. The play on words with* lost *and* laced *was meant to be clever and humorous.*

PROTEUS
> The world isn't big enough for all these damn sheep.

SPEED
> If it's too crowded for you, then you should stick her.

PROTEUS
> No, now you've really gone astray. I ought to pound you.

SPEED
> No, sir, less than a pound will suffice for delivering your letter.

PROTEUS
> You misunderstood. I meant *give you a pounding, pinhead.*

SPEED
> You've gone from a pound down to a pinhead? No, I want more than that—that's far too little payment for delivering a letter to your lover.

PROTEUS
> So what did she say?

SPEED
> *(nodding)* Ay.

PROTEUS
> Nod-ay? Well, that's "naughty."

SPEED
> You misunderstood, sir. I said she nodded, and you asked me if she nodded, and I said, "Ay."

PROTEUS
> And all that put together is "naughty."

SPEED
Now you have taken the pains to set it together, take it for your pains.

PROTEUS
No, no, you shall have it for bearing the letter.

SPEED
Well, I perceive I must be fain to bear with you.

PROTEUS
Why, sir, how do you bear with me?

SPEED
Marry, sir, the letter, very orderly, having nothing but the word "noddy" for my pains.

PROTEUS
Beshrew me, but you have a quick wit.

SPEED
And yet it cannot overtake your slow purse.

PROTEUS
Come, come, open the matter in brief. What said she?

SPEED
Open your purse, that the money and the matter may be both at once delivered.

PROTEUS
(*Giving him money*) Well, sir, here is for your pains. What said she?

SPEED
Truly, sir, I think you'll hardly win her.

PROTEUS
Why, couldst thou perceive so much from her?

SPEED
Sir, I could perceive nothing at all from her, no, not so much as a ducat for delivering your letter. And being so hard to me that brought your mind, I fear she'll prove as hard to you in telling your mind. Give her no token but stones, for she's as hard as steel.

PROTEUS
What said she? Nothing?

ACT 1, SCENE 1

NO FEAR SHAKESPEARE

SPEED

Now that you've taken the trouble to figure it out, take that for your trouble and consider it your answer.

PROTEUS

No, no, you shall have it for delivering the letter.

SPEED

Well, I guess I must be willing to put up with you.

PROTEUS

Why, sir, what do you mean, "put up with me"?

SPEED

Geez, sir, I mean getting nothing but the word "naughty" as payment for my delivery.

PROTEUS

Damn, you have a quick wit.

SPEED

And yet I can't speed past your slowness in paying me.

PROTEUS

Come on, come on, tell me briefly. What did she say?

SPEED

Open your wallet, and the money and her response will both be delivered.

PROTEUS

(*Giving him money*) Well, sir, here's something for your trouble. What did she say?

SPEED

Honestly, sir, I think you'll have a hard time winning her.

PROTEUS

Why? Did you get that from speaking with her?

SPEED

Sir, I couldn't get anything at all out of her, not even so much as a tip for delivering your letter. And since she was so stingy to me for having delivered your thoughts, I fear she'll prove just as stingy with you. Don't give her any little gifts except stones, because she's as hard as steel.

PROTEUS

What did she say? Nothing?

SPEED
> No, not so much as "Take this for thy pains." To testify
> your bounty, I thank you, you have testerned me; in
> requital whereof, henceforth carry your letters yourself.
> And so, sir, I'll commend you to my master.

PROTEUS
> Go, go, begone, to save your ship from wreck,
> Which cannot perish having thee aboard,
> Being destined to a drier death on shore.

Exit SPEED

> I must go send some better messenger.
> I fear my Julia would not deign my lines,
> Receiving them from such a worthless post.

Exit

ACT 1, SCENE 1
NO FEAR SHAKESPEARE

SPEED

> No, not even so much as "Take this for your trouble."
> I can attest to your generosity since you've given me a
> small tip. In return, you can deliver your own letters from
> now on. And so, sir, I'll say hello to my master for you.

PROTEUS

> Go on, get out of here. You'll save your ship from
> destruction **since you're destined to die on
> dry land**.
>
> *SPEED exits.*

Refers to the saying "He that is born to be hanged shall never be drowned."

> I must send a letter with a better messenger. I'm
> afraid my Julia wouldn't accept my letter because she
> received it from such a worthless postman.
>
> *PROTEUS exits.*

ACT 1, SCENE 2

Enter JULIA *and* LUCETTA

JULIA
But say, Lucetta, now we are alone,
Wouldst thou then counsel me to fall in love?

LUCETTA
Ay, madam, so you stumble not unheedfully.

JULIA
Of all the fair resort of gentlemen
That every day with parle encounter me,
In thy opinion which is worthiest love?

LUCETTA
Please you repeat their names, I'll show my mind
According to my shallow simple skill.

JULIA
What think'st thou of the fair Sir Eglamour?

LUCETTA
As of a knight well-spoken, neat, and fine;
But, were I you, he never should be mine.

JULIA
What think'st thou of the rich Mercatio?

LUCETTA
Well of his wealth, but of himself, so-so.

JULIA
What think'st thou of the gentle Proteus?

LUCETTA
Lord, Lord, to see what folly reigns in us!

JULIA
How now? What means this passion at his name?

LUCETTA
Pardon, dear madam, 'tis a passing shame
That I, unworthy body as I am,
Should censure thus on lovely gentlemen.

ACT 1, SCENE 2

JULIA *and* LUCETTA *enter.*

JULIA
Now that we're alone, tell me, Lucetta, would you recommend that I fall in love?

LUCETTA
Yes, madame, so you stumble into it on purpose.

JULIA
Of all the attractive gentlemen that speak with me daily, which do you think would be best to love?

LUCETTA
Please tell me their names again, and I'll tell you my opinion about them as best I can.

JULIA
What do you think of the attractive Sir Eglamour?

LUCETTA
As a knight, he's well-spoken, elegant, and fine. But if I were you, I wouldn't fall in love with him.

JULIA
What do you think of Mercatio, who is rich?

LUCETTA
I like his money a lot, but him only so-so.

JULIA
What do you think of kind Proteus?

LUCETTA
Good Lord, how foolish people are!

JULIA
What's that for? Why this outburst at his name?

LUCETTA
Pardon me, dear madame, it's inexcusable that I, the unworthy servant that I am, should criticize such lovely gentlemen.

JULIA
Why not on Proteus, as of all the rest?

LUCETTA
Then thus, of many good I think him best.

JULIA
Your reason?

LUCETTA
I have no other but a woman's reason;
I think him so because I think him so.

JULIA
And wouldst thou have me cast my love on him?

LUCETTA
Ay, if you thought your love not cast away.

JULIA
Why, he of all the rest hath never moved me.

LUCETTA
Yet he of all the rest I think best loves ye.

JULIA
His little speaking shows his love but small.

LUCETTA
Fire that's closest kept burns most of all.

JULIA
They do not love that do not show their love.

LUCETTA
O, they love least that let men know their love.

JULIA
I would I knew his mind.

LUCETTA
(*Giving a letter*)   Peruse this paper, madam.

JULIA
(*Reads*) "To Julia." Say, from whom?

LUCETTA
That the contents will show.

JULIA
Say, say, who gave it thee?

ACT 1, SCENE 2
NO FEAR SHAKESPEARE

JULIA
> Why don't you think well of Proteus out of all the rest?

LUCETTA
> Fine then—of all the good men, I think Proteus is best.

JULIA
> What's your reason?

LUCETTA
> I have no other reason than a woman's intuition: I think he's the best simply because I do.

JULIA
> And would you have me throw my love at him?

LUCETTA
> Yes, if you thought your love wouldn't be thrown away.

JULIA
> But, of all the others, he has never proposed to me.

LUCETTA
> Yet, of all the others, I think he loves you the most.

JULIA
> The fact that he doesn't say much to me shows he doesn't love me much.

LUCETTA
> Fire that's most enclosed burns most of all.

JULIA
> Those who don't show their love don't love at all.

LUCETTA
> Oh, those who tell others of their love love the least of all.

JULIA
> I wish I knew how he felt.

LUCETTA
> (*Giving her a letter*) Read this paper, madame.

JULIA
> "To Julia." Tell me, who's it from?

LUCETTA
> The letter will say.

JULIA
> Tell me, who gave it to you?

MODERN TEXT

Two Gentlemen of Verona   Act 1, Scene

LUCETTA
    Sir Valentine's page; and sent, I think, from Proteus.
    He would have given it you, but I, being in the way,
40   Did in your name receive it. Pardon the fault, I pray.

JULIA
    Now, by my modesty, a goodly broker!
    Dare you presume to harbor wanton lines?
    To whisper and conspire against my youth?
    Now trust me, 'tis an office of great worth,
45   And you an officer fit for the place.
    There, take the paper. See it be returned,
    Or else return no more into my sight.

(Giving the letter back)

LUCETTA
    To plead for love deserves more fee than hate.

JULIA
    Will ye be gone?

LUCETTA
50   That you may ruminate.

Exit

JULIA
    And yet I would I had o'erlooked the letter.
    It were a shame to call her back again
    And pray her to a fault for which I chid her.
    What fool is she, that knows I am a maid
55   And would not force the letter to my view!
    Since maids, in modesty, say no to that
    Which they would have the profferer construe ay.
    Fie, fie, how wayward is this foolish love
    That, like a testy babe, will scratch the nurse
60   And presently, all humbled, kiss the rod!
    How churlishly I chid Lucetta hence,
    When willingly I would have had her here!
    How angerly I taught my brow to frown,
    When inward joy enforced my heart to smile!

ACT 1, SCENE 2
NO FEAR SHAKESPEARE

LUCETTA

Sir Valentine's servant, but I think it was sent from Proteus. He would have given it to you himself, but I ran into him first and took it in your name. Please forgive me.

JULIA

Well, you're a fine go-between! Do you dare receive love letters, and to whisper and conspire against me because of my lack of experience? Trust me, it's an important job, and you're just the kind of person for it. There, take the letter. See that it's returned, or else don't let me see you again.

(Giving the letter back)

LUCETTA

A request for your love deserves more in return than your hatred.

JULIA

Will you get going?

LUCETTA

Just think about it.

LUCETTA exits.

JULIA

Then again, I wish I had read the letter. It would be embarrassing to call her back again and do the very thing I chided her for. How foolish she is, since she knows I'm a single girl but still wouldn't make me read it! Out of modesty girls say "no" when they wish the giver would construe it as "yes." How difficult this foolish thing called love is, like a cranky baby that will scratch its nurse and then immediately after show affection. How rudely I scolded Lucetta, when really I wanted her here. I've taught myself to appear angry even when my heart smiles with joy! My punishment is to call Lucetta back and ask forgiveness for my mistake. Hey, Lucetta!

65 My penance is to call Lucetta back
And ask remission for my folly past.
What ho! Lucetta!

Enter LUCETTA

LUCETTA
What would your ladyship?
JULIA
Is't near dinner time?
LUCETTA
70 I would it were,
That you might kill your stomach on your meat
And not upon your maid.
(She drops the letter and stoops to pick it up.)
JULIA
What is't that you took up so gingerly?
LUCETTA
Nothing.
JULIA
75 Why didst thou stoop, then?
LUCETTA
To take a paper up that I let fall.
JULIA
And is that paper nothing?
LUCETTA
Nothing concerning me.
JULIA
Then let it lie for those that it concerns.
LUCETTA
80 Madam, it will not lie where it concerns,
Unless it have a false interpreter.
JULIA
Some love of yours hath writ to you in rhyme.

ACT 1, SCENE 2

NO FEAR SHAKESPEARE

LUCETTA *enters.*

LUCETTA
What would you like, my lady?

JULIA
Is it almost dinnertime?

LUCETTA
I wish it were, so that you could chew on your food instead of your servant.
(She drops the letter and stoops to pick it up.)

JULIA
What is that that you picked up so carefully?

LUCETTA
Nothing.

JULIA
Why did you bend over, then?

LUCETTA
To pick up the paper that I dropped.

JULIA
And that paper is nothing?

LUCETTA
Nothing that concerns me.

JULIA
Then let it lie on the ground for the people it does concern.

LUCETTA
Madame, it will not lie about what it concerns unless a liar reads it.

JULIA
Some lover of yours has written a poem to you.

LUCETTA
>That I might sing it, madam, to a tune,
>Give me a note; your ladyship can set.

JULIA
85 As little by such toys as may be possible.
Best sing it to the tune of "Light o' Love."

LUCETTA
>It is too heavy for so light a tune.

JULIA
>Heavy! Belike it hath some burden then?

LUCETTA
>Ay, and melodious were it, would you sing it.

JULIA
90 And why not you?

LUCETTA
>I cannot reach so high.

JULIA
>Let's see your song. How now, minion?

(She takes the letter.)

LUCETTA
>Keep tune there still; so you will sing it out.
>And yet methinks I do not like this tune.

JULIA
95 You do not?

LUCETTA
>No, madam, 'tis too sharp.

JULIA
>You, minion, are too saucy.

LUCETTA
>Nay, now you are too flat,
>And mar the concord with too harsh a descant.
100 There wanteth but a mean to fill your song.

JULIA
>The mean is drowned with your unruly bass.

LUCETTA
>Indeed, I bid the base for Proteus.

ACT 1, SCENE 2
NO FEAR SHAKESPEARE

LUCETTA
> I'll sing it, madame, to a tune. Give me the note to sing it in. Your ladyship can choose it.

JULIA
> I place as little value as possible in such trifles. You should sing it to the tune of "Light o' Love."

LUCETTA
> The poem is too heavy for so light a tune.

JULIA
> Too heavy! I guess the note is serious, then?

LUCETTA
> Yes, and it would be melodious, too, if you'd sing it.

JULIA
> And why won't *you* sing it?

LUCETTA
> I cannot reach such high notes.

JULIA
> Let's see your poem. What is it, you hussy?
> *(She takes the letter.)*

LUCETTA
> Keep your mood in check and get over your anger. I don't like this new tune you're singing.

JULIA
> You don't?

LUCETTA
> No, madame, it's too sharp.

JULIA
> You, hussy, are too sassy.

LUCETTA
> No, now you're too flat. You're ruining the harmony with a melody that's too harsh. Your song only needs a **tenor**.

In other words, Julia needs a man.

JULIA
> The tenor is ruined with your unruly bass.

LUCETTA
> Indeed, I sing for Proteus.

JULIA
    This babble shall not henceforth trouble me.
    Here is a coil with protestation!
    (*She tears the letter and drops the pieces.*)
    Go, get you gone, and let the papers lie.
    You would be fing'ring them to anger me.

LUCETTA
    She makes it strange, but she would be best pleased
    To be so angered with another letter.

Exit

JULIA
    Nay, would I were so angered with the same!
    (*She picks up some fragments.*)
    O hateful hands, to tear such loving words!
    Injurious wasps, to feed on such sweet honey
    And kill the bees that yield it with your stings!
    I'll kiss each several paper for amends.
    Look, here is writ "kind Julia." Unkind Julia!
    As in revenge of thy ingratitude,
    I throw thy name against the bruising stones,
    Trampling contemptuously on thy disdain.
    (*She throws down a fragment.*)
    And here is writ "love-wounded Proteus."
    Poor wounded name! My bosom as a bed
    Shall lodge thee till thy wound be throughly healed;
    And thus I search it with a sovereign kiss.
    But twice or thrice was "Proteus" written down.
    Be calm, good wind, blow not a word away
    Till I have found each letter in the letter,
    Except mine own name; that some whirlwind bear
    Unto a ragged, fearful, hanging rock
    And throw it thence into the raging sea!
    Lo, here in one line is his name twice writ,
    "Poor forlorn Proteus, passionate Proteus,
    To the sweet Julia." That I'll tear away;
    And yet I will not, sith so prettily

ACT 1, SCENE 2
NO FEAR SHAKESPEARE

JULIA

> This letter won't trouble me from now on. Here's a fuss over a love letter!
> (*She tears the letter and drops the pieces.*)
> Go, get out of here, and leave the papers where they are. I know you'd try to pick them up just to anger me.

LUCETTA

> She pretends not to care, but she would be happy to be so angered by another love letter.

LUCETTA exits.

JULIA

> No, I wish I were so angry with this one!
> (*She picks up some fragments.*)
> Stupid hands, to tear up such lovely words! Destructive fingers, to feed on such sweet words and then rip up the letter they came from! I'll apologize by kissing each piece of paper. Here, this one says "kind Julia." It should say "unkind Julia!" Out of revenge for my own ingratitude I'll throw the paper on the floor and hatefully trample my name in disdain.
> (*She throws down a fragment.*)
> And here's one that says "love-wounded Proteus." Poor wounded name! My breast will serve as your bed until your wounds are completely healed. I cleanse them with a healing kiss. But "Proteus" was written down two or three times. Be still, good wind, and don't blow these pieces of paper away until I've found each word in the letter, except for the piece with my own name on it—may some whirlwind take that piece, hurl it onto a frightening cliff, and from there throw it into the raging sea! Look, his name is written twice in this line: "Poor forlorn Proteus, passionate Proteus, to the sweet Julia." I'll tear that last part off. Then again, maybe I won't, since he tied

135   He couples it to his complaining names.
Thus will I fold them, one upon another.
Now kiss, embrace, contend, do what you will.
(She puts some folded papers in her bosom.)

Enter LUCETTA

LUCETTA
Madam, dinner is ready, and your father stays.
JULIA
Well, let us go.
LUCETTA
140   What, shall these papers lie like telltales here?

JULIA
If you respect them, best to take them up.

LUCETTA
Nay, I was taken up for laying them down;
Yet here they shall not lie, for catching cold.
(She gathers up the remaining fragments.)
JULIA
I see you have a month's mind to them.
LUCETTA
145   Ay, madam, you may say what sights you see;
I see things too, although you judge I wink.

JULIA
Come, come; will 't please you go?

Exeunt

ACT 1, SCENE 2
NO FEAR SHAKESPEARE

it so prettily to his own sorrowful names. I'll fold them up, one on top of another. Now the names may kiss, hug, battle, or do what they will.

(She puts some folded papers in her shirt.)

LUCETTA *enters.*

LUCETTA
Madame, dinner is ready, and your father waits for you.

JULIA
Well, let's go then.

LUCETTA
What, should these papers just lie on the ground revealing everything?

JULIA
If you respect them, then it would be best to pick them up.

LUCETTA
No, you yelled at me for dropping them in the first place. But we shouldn't leave them here or they'll catch a cold.
(She gathers up the remaining fragments.)

JULIA
I see you have a strong desire for them.

LUCETTA
Yes, madame, you can interpret my behavior as you like. But I see things, too, even though you think my eyes are closed.

JULIA
Come on, come on. Will you please hurry up?

They exit.

ACT 1, SCENE 3

Enter ANTONIO *and* PANTHINO

ANTONIO
    Tell me, Panthino, what sad talk was that
    Wherewith my brother held you in the cloister?

PANTHINO
    'Twas of his nephew Proteus, your son.

ANTONIO
    Why, what of him?

PANTHINO
                      He wondered that your lordship
    Would suffer him to spend his youth at home,
    While other men, of slender reputation,
    Put forth their sons to seek preferment out,
    Some to the wars, to try their fortune there,
    Some to discover islands far away,
    Some to the studious universities.
    For any or for all these exercises
    He said that Proteus your son was meet,
    And did request me to importune you
    To let him spend his time no more at home,
    Which would be great impeachment to his age
    In having known no travel in his youth.

ANTONIO
    Nor need'st thou much importune me to that
    Whereon this month I have been hammering.
    I have considered well his loss of time,
    And how he cannot be a perfect man,
    Not being tried and tutored in the world.
    Experience is by industry achieved
    And perfected by the swift course of time.
    Then tell me, whither were I best to send him?

ACT 1, SCENE 3

ANTONIO *and* PANTHINO *enter.*

ANTONIO
Tell me, Panthino, what were you and my brother talking so seriously about in the walkway back there?

PANTHINO
We were talking about his nephew, your son, Proteus.

ANTONIO
Why? What about him?

PANTHINO
He wondered why your lordship would let him spend his youth here at home. Other men with lesser reputations send their sons to seek opportunities abroad, or to find their fortunes fighting in the wars, or to discover faraway islands, or to study in the universities. He said that Proteus was capable of doing any or all of these things, and he asked me to urge you not to let him spend any more time at home. It would be a shame for him in old age not to have traveled in his youth.

ANTONIO
You don't need to urge me on this matter. I've thought about it a lot this month. I've considered how much time he's wasting, and how he cannot be a complete man without having some real-world trials and tests. Experience comes from hard work and is perfected over the course of time. Tell me, though, where would it be best to send him?

PANTHINO
>I think your lordship is not ignorant
>How his companion, youthful Valentine,
>Attends the Emperor in his royal court.

ANTONIO
>I know it well.

PANTHINO
>'Twere good, I think, your lordship sent him thither.
>There shall he practice tilts and tournaments,
>Hear sweet discourse, converse with noblemen,
>And be in eye of every exercise
>Worthy his youth and nobleness of birth.

ANTONIO
>I like thy counsel; well hast thou advised;
>And that thou mayst perceive how well I like it,
>The execution of it shall make known.
>Even with the speediest expedition
>I will dispatch him to the Emperor's court.

PANTHINO
>Tomorrow, may it please you, Don Alphonso
>With other gentlemen of good esteem
>Are journeying to salute the Emperor
>And to commend their service to his will.

ANTONIO
>Good company. With them shall Proteus go—

Enter **PROTEUS**, *reading a letter.*

>And in good time! Now will we break with him.

PROTEUS
>(*To himself*) Sweet love, sweet lines, sweet life!
>Here is her hand, the agent of her heart;
>Here is her oath for love, her honor's pawn.
>O that our fathers would applaud our loves,
>To seal our happiness with their consents!
>O heavenly Julia!

ACT 1, SCENE 3
NO FEAR SHAKESPEARE

PANTHINO

> I think your lordship knows that his friend, the young Valentine, has gone off to visit the emperor in his royal court in Milan.

ANTONIO

> I'm fully aware.

PANTHINO

> It would be good, I think, if your lordship sent him there. There he can take part in jousts and tournaments, listen to learned discussions, speak with noblemen, and witness everything befitting his youth and nobleness of birth.

ANTONIO

> I like what you say. You've advised me well. And so you may see how much I like it, I'll announce it publicly. I'll send him off to the emperor's court immediately.

PANTHINO

> May it please you, Don Alphonso and some other noblemen are setting off tomorrow to visit the emperor and to offer their services to help him in whatever he needs.

ANTONIO

> Sounds like a good group. Proteus will go with them.

PROTEUS enters, reading a letter.

> Just in time! I'll talk to him now.

PROTEUS

> (*To himself*) Sweet love, sweet poetry, sweet life! Here is a letter in her handwriting, which does the bidding of her heart. Here is her pledge of love, which vows she will be faithful. Oh, I wish our fathers would approve of our love and consent to let us marry, sealing our happiness forever. Oh, heavenly Julia!

MODERN TEXT

Two Gentlemen of Verona   Act 1, Scene 3

ANTONIO
>How now? What letter are you reading there?

PROTEUS
>May't please your lordship, 'tis a word or two
>Of commendations sent from Valentine,
>Delivered by a friend that came from him.

ANTONIO
>Lend me the letter. Let me see what news.

PROTEUS
>There is no news, my lord, but that he writes
>How happily he lives, how well beloved
>And daily gracèd by the Emperor;
>Wishing me with him, partner of his fortune.

ANTONIO
>And how stand you affected to his wish?

PROTEUS
>As one relying on your lordship's will,
>And not depending on his friendly wish.

ANTONIO
>My will is something sorted with his wish.
>Muse not that I thus suddenly proceed,
>For what I will, I will, and there an end.
>I am resolved that thou shalt spend some time
>With Valentinus in the Emperor's court.
>What maintenance he from his friends receives,
>Like exhibition thou shalt have from me.
>Tomorrow be in readiness to go.
>Excuse it not, for I am peremptory.

PROTEUS
>My lord, I cannot be so soon provided.
>Please you, deliberate a day or two.

ANTONIO
>Look what thou want'st shall be sent after thee.
>No more of stay. Tomorrow thou must go.
>Come on, Panthino; you shall be employed
>To hasten on his expedition.

Exeunt **ANTONIO** *and* **PANTHINO**

ACT 1, SCENE 3

NO FEAR SHAKESPEARE

ANTONIO

> What's that you say? What's that letter you're reading there?

PROTEUS

> Your lordship, it's just a short note of greeting from Valentine, delivered to me by a friend of his.

ANTONIO

> Give me the letter. Let me see what news it brings.

PROTEUS

> There is no news, my lord. He just writes how happy he is and that the emperor likes him and honors him each day. He wishes I were with him to share his good luck.

ANTONIO

> And how do you feel about his wish?

PROTEUS

> Like one who is used to following your orders and not able to honor Valentine's wishes.

ANTONIO

> My wish is similar to Valentine's. Now don't think that I decided this rashly, because I get what I want, and that's final. I've decided that you should spend some time with Valentine in the emperor's court. I'll provide you with the same money for room and board that he receives from his family. Be ready to go tomorrow. Don't try to get out of it now, because I've made up my mind.

PROTEUS

> My lord, I can't get ready that quickly. Please, think about this a day or two longer.

ANTONIO

> Look, whatever you want will be sent to you after you leave. You're not going to stay here any longer. You must go tomorrow. Come on, Panthino, you will help get everything ready so he can leave as soon as possible.
>
> > > > > > > > > > > **ANTONIO** *and* **PANTHINO** *exit.*

MODERN TEXT

PROTEUS

>Thus have I shunned the fire for fear of burning,
>And drenched me in the sea, where I am drowned.
>I feared to show my father Julia's letter
>Lest he should take exceptions to my love,
>And with the vantage of mine own excuse
>Hath he excepted most against my love.
>O! how this spring of love resembleth
>The uncertain glory of an April day,
>Which now shows all the beauty of the sun,
>And by and by a cloud takes all away!

Enter PANTHINO.

PANTHINO

>Sir Proteus, your father calls for you.
>He is in haste; therefore, I pray you, go.

PROTEUS

>Why, this it is: my heart accords thereto,
>And yet a thousand times it answers no.

Exeunt

ACT 1, SCENE 3
NO FEAR SHAKESPEARE

PROTEUS

> I dove into the sea to avoid being burned by the fire, and now I'm drowning instead. I was afraid to show Julia's letter to my father because I didn't want him to disapprove of my love, but taking advantage of my lie he raised more obstacles against it. Oh, our new love is like the uncertain days of April, which will be sunny one moment, and suddenly a cloud takes the sunshine away!

PANTHINO enters.

PANTHINO

> Sir Proteus, your father calls for you. He's in a hurry, so I beg you, go quickly.

PROTEUS

> This is how it is: my heart agrees to it but wants to say no a thousand times.

They exit.

ACT TWO
SCENE 1

Enter VALENTINE *and* SPEED

SPEED
Sir, your glove.

(He offers a glove.)

VALENTINE
Not mine. My gloves are on.

SPEED
Why, then, this may be yours, for this is but one.

VALENTINE
Ha! let me see. Ay, give it me, it's mine.
Sweet ornament that decks a thing divine!
Ah, Sylvia, Sylvia!

SPEED
(*Calling*) Madam Sylvia! Madam Sylvia!

VALENTINE
How now, sirrah?

SPEED
She is not within hearing, sir.

VALENTINE
Why, sir, who bade you call her?

SPEED
Your worship, sir, or else I mistook.

VALENTINE
Well, you'll still be too forward.

SPEED
And yet I was last chidden for being too slow.

VALENTINE
Go to, sir. Tell me, do you know Madam Sylvia?

SPEED
She that your worship loves?

ACT TWO
SCENE 1

VALENTINE *and* SPEED *enter.*

SPEED
Sir, here is your glove.

(He offers a glove.)

VALENTINE
That isn't mine. I'm already wearing my gloves.

SPEED
Well, then, this may be your glove, because it's all by itself.

VALENTINE
Ha! Let me see it. Yes, give it to me. It's mine. Sweet accessory that Sylvia's divine hand wears. Ah Sylvia, Sylvia!

SPEED
(*Calling*) Madame Sylvia! Madame Sylvia!

VALENTINE
What are you doing, **pal**?

> Sirrah, *the word used in Shakespeare's original language, is used to address a social inferior.*

SPEED
She's too far away to hear me, sir.

VALENTINE
But, sir, who asked you to call out for her?

SPEED
You did, sir, or else I misunderstood you.

VALENTINE
Well, you're always too presumptuous.

SPEED
Even though last time I was scolded for being too slow.

VALENTINE
Enough, sir. Tell me, do you know Madame Sylvia?

SPEED
The Madame Sylvia you love, your worship?

MODERN TEXT

VALENTINE
  Why, how know you that I am in love?
SPEED
  Marry, by these special marks: first, you have learned,
  like Sir Proteus, to wreath your arms, like a malcontent;
  to relish a love-song, like a robin redbreast; to walk alone,
  like one that had the pestilence; to sigh, like a schoolboy
  that had lost his A B C; to weep, like a young wench that
  had buried her grandam; to fast, like one that takes diet;
  to watch, like one that fears robbing; to speak puling,
  like a beggar at Hallowmas. You were wont, when you
  laughed, to crow like a cock; when you walked, to walk
  like one of the lions; when you fasted, it was presently
  after dinner; when you looked sadly, it was for want
  of money. And now you are metamorphosed with a
  mistress, that when I look on you, I can hardly think you
  my master.

VALENTINE
  Are all these things perceived in me?
SPEED
  They are all perceived without ye.
VALENTINE
  Without me? They cannot.
SPEED
  Without you? Nay, that's certain, for, without you were
  so simple, none else would. But you are so without these
  follies that these follies are within you, and shine through
  you like the water in an urinal, that not an eye that sees
  you but is a physician to comment on your malady.

VALENTINE
  But tell me, dost thou know my lady Sylvia?
SPEED
  She that you gaze on so as she sits at supper?

ACT 2, SCENE 1
NO FEAR SHAKESPEARE

VALENTINE
> Why, how do you know that I am in love?

SPEED
> Because of all the right signs, of course: First, like Sir Proteus, you have started to fold your arms like you're unhappy about something. You go around singing love songs like a red-breasted robin. You walk alone like one who has the plague. You sigh like a schoolboy who has lost his textbook. You weep like a young girl who has just buried her grandmother. You don't eat, like one who's on a diet. You can't sleep, like one who fears being robbed. You whine like a beggar on **Hallowmas.** It used to be that when you laughed, you crowed like a rooster. When you walked, you walked like a lion. When you didn't eat, it was because you'd just finished lunch. When you looked sad, it was because you were out of money. And now a mistress has changed you. When I look at you, I can hardly recognize you as my master.

Hallowmas, or All Saint's Day, took place on November 1, and it was customary on that day to give charity to beggars.

VALENTINE
> Can you see all these things in me?

SPEED
> They are all outside of you, in your outward appearance.

VALENTINE
> Outside of me? They cannot be outside of me.

SPEED
> Outside of you? No, I'm sure, because if you weren't so obvious no one would see them. But your appearance is so marked by these foolish traits that they must be inside you, and they shine through you as if you were water in a jar. Everyone that sees you is like a physician who knows why you're sick.

VALENTINE
> But tell me, do you know my lady Sylvia?

SPEED
> The woman you stare at while she sits at the dinner table?

MODERN TEXT

VALENTINE
>Hast thou observed that? Even she I mean.

SPEED
>Why, sir, I know her not.

VALENTINE
>Dost thou know her by my gazing on her, and yet know'st her not?

SPEED
>45 Is she not hard-favored, sir?

VALENTINE
>Not so fair, boy, as well-favored.

SPEED
>Sir, I know that well enough.

VALENTINE
>What dost thou know?

SPEED
>That she is not so fair as, of you, well-favored.

VALENTINE
>50 I mean that her beauty is exquisite but her favor infinite.

SPEED
>That's because the one is painted and the other out of all count.

VALENTINE
>How painted? And how out of count?

SPEED
>Marry, sir, so painted, to make her fair, that no man
>55 counts of her beauty.

VALENTINE
>How esteem'st thou me? I account of her beauty.

SPEED
>You never saw her since she was deformed.

ACT 2, SCENE 1
NO FEAR SHAKESPEARE

VALENTINE
> Have you noticed me doing that? Yes, that's the woman I mean.

SPEED
> Well, sir, I don't know her at all.

VALENTINE
> Do you know her only by my staring at her and not otherwise?

SPEED
> Isn't she ugly, sir?

VALENTINE
> She's not as beautiful, boy, as she is gracious.

SPEED
> Sir, I know that very well.

VALENTINE
> What do you know?

SPEED
> That she isn't as pretty as she is looked on favorably by you.

VALENTINE
> I mean that her beauty is exquisite but her graciousness is infinite.

SPEED
> That's because the first one is done with makeup and the other can't be counted.

VALENTINE
> What do you mean, done with makeup? And why can't you count the other?

SPEED
> I mean, sir, she's so painted with makeup to look beautiful that no man values her beauty.

VALENTINE
> So what do you think of me, then? I think she's very beautiful.

SPEED
> You haven't seen her since she was deformed.

MODERN TEXT

VALENTINE
How long hath she been deformed?

SPEED
Ever since you loved her.

VALENTINE
I have loved her ever since I saw her, and still I see her beautiful.

SPEED
If you love her, you cannot see her.

VALENTINE
Why?

SPEED
Because Love is blind. O, that you had mine eyes, or your own eyes had the lights they were wont to have when you chid at Sir Proteus for going ungartered!

VALENTINE
What should I see then?

SPEED
Your own present folly and her passing deformity; for he, being in love, could not see to garter his hose, and you, being in love, cannot see to put on your hose.

VALENTINE
Belike, boy, then you are in love, for last morning you could not see to wipe my shoes.

SPEED
True, sir. I was in love with my bed. I thank you, you swinged me for my love, which makes me the bolder to chide you for yours.

VALENTINE
In conclusion, I stand affected to her.

SPEED
I would you were set; so your affection would cease.

ACT 2, SCENE 1
NO FEAR SHAKESPEARE

VALENTINE
> How long has she been deformed?

SPEED
> Ever since you fell in love with her.

VALENTINE
> I have loved her ever since I first saw her, and I still think she's beautiful.

SPEED
> If you love her then you cannot see her.

VALENTINE
> Why not?

SPEED
> Because Love is blind. Oh, if you had my eyes, or if you could see as clearly as you did when you scolded Sir Proteus for **not wearing a garter**!

Garters were used to keep stockings from falling, and going without garters was popularly considered a sign of lovesickness.

VALENTINE
> What would I see then?

SPEED
> Your own current foolishness and her enormous deformity. Proteus, because he was in love, forgot to put on a garter to keep his stockings up, and you, also being in love, can't see well enough to even put on your stockings.

VALENTINE
> Then maybe, boy, you're in love, because this morning you couldn't see well enough to polish my shoes.

SPEED
> True, sir. I was in love with my bed. I thank you—you hit me because I was so in love, which has made me bold enough to scold you for your love.

VALENTINE
> In conclusion, I'm in love with her.

SPEED
> I wish you weren't standing erect. Maybe then your love would go away.

VALENTINE
>Last night she enjoined me to write some lines to one she loves.

SPEED
>And have you?

VALENTINE
>I have.

SPEED
>Are they not lamely writ?

VALENTINE
>No, boy, but as well as I can do them. Peace, here she comes.

Enter SYLVIA.

SPEED
>(*Aside*) O, excellent motion! O, exceeding puppet! Now will he interpret to her.

VALENTINE
>Madam and mistress, a thousand good-morrows.

SPEED
>(*Aside*) O! give ye good even! Here's a million of manners.

SYLVIA
>Sir Valentine and servant, to you two thousand.

SPEED
>(*Aside*) He should give her interest, and she gives it him.

VALENTINE
>As you enjoined me, I have writ your letter
>Unto the secret, nameless friend of yours,
>Which I was much unwilling to proceed in
>But for my duty to your ladyship.

>>*(He gives* SYLVIA *a letter.)*

ACT 2, SCENE 1
NO FEAR SHAKESPEARE

VALENTINE

Last night she asked me to write some lines of poetry to the one she loves.

SPEED

And did you?

VALENTINE

I did.

SPEED

They're badly written, aren't they?

VALENTINE

No, boy, I wrote them as well as I could. Be quiet now—here she comes.

SYLVIA enters.

SPEED

(*Aside*) Oh, what a puppet show! Such a wonderful puppet she makes. Now he'll give his commentary on the show.

VALENTINE

Madame and mistress, I wish you a thousand good mornings.

SPEED

(*Aside*) And God give you a good evening! What manners!

SYLVIA

Sir Valentine and servant, to you I wish two thousand good mornings.

SPEED

(*Aside*) He should outdo her in compliments, but she outdoes him.

VALENTINE

As you asked, I have written your letter to that secret, anonymous friend of yours. Though I didn't want to do it, I wrote it out of duty to your ladyship.

(He gives SYLVIA a letter.)

MODERN TEXT

SYLVIA
I thank you, gentle servant. 'Tis very clerkly done.
VALENTINE
Now trust me, madam, it came hardly off;
For, being ignorant to whom it goes,
I writ at random, very doubtfully.
SYLVIA
Perchance you think too much of so much pains?
VALENTINE
No, madam. So it stead you, I will write—
Please you command—a thousand times as much.
And yet—
SYLVIA
A pretty period! Well, I guess the sequel;
And yet I will not name it—and yet I care not—
And yet take this again—and yet I thank you,
Meaning henceforth to trouble you no more.

(She offers him the letter.)

SPEED
(Aside) And yet you will, and yet another "yet."
VALENTINE
What means your ladyship? Do you not like it?
SYLVIA
Yes, yes. The lines are very quaintly writ,
But, since unwillingly, take them again.
Nay, take them.

(She gives back the letter.)

VALENTINE
Madam, they are for you.
SYLVIA
Ay, ay. You writ them, sir, at my request,
But I will none of them. They are for you.
I would have had them writ more movingly.
VALENTINE
Please you, I'll write your ladyship another.

ACT 2, SCENE 1
NO FEAR SHAKESPEARE

SYLVIA
> I thank you, gentle servant. It's very smartly written.

VALENTINE
> Now trust me, madame, it wasn't easy to write this, because I had to be somewhat vague since I didn't know to whom it would go.

SYLVIA
> Perhaps you think it was too much trouble?

VALENTINE
> No, madame. If it helps you, I will write a thousand times as many lines if you like. And yet . . .

SYLVIA
> A fine pause! I can guess what you're going to say next. And yet I will not say it. And yet I don't care. And yet you can take this back. And yet thanks anyway, meaning I won't bother you again.
>
> *(She offers him the letter.)*

SPEED
> (*Aside*) And yet you will, and yet say another "yet."

VALENTINE
> What do you mean, your ladyship? Don't you like it?

SYLVIA
> Yes, yes. The lines are very nicely written, but since you wrote them so unwillingly, take them back. No, take them.
>
> *(She gives back the letter.)*

VALENTINE
> Madame, they are for you.

SYLVIA
> Yes, yes. You wrote them, sir, at my request, but I don't want them. They are for you. I wish they had been more movingly written.

VALENTINE
> If it pleases you, I'll write another for your ladyship.

SYLVIA
　　And when it's writ, for my sake read it over.
　　And if it please you, so; if not, why, so.
VALENTINE
　　If it please me, madam, what then?
SYLVIA
120　Why, if it please you, take it for your labor.
　　And so good morrow, servant.

Exit SYLVIA

SPEED
　　(*Aside*) O jest unseen, inscrutable, invisible
　　As a nose on a man's face or a weathercock on a steeple!
　　My master sues to her, and she hath taught her suitor,
125　He being her pupil, to become her tutor.
　　O excellent device! Was there ever heard a better,
　　That my master, being scribe, to himself should write
　　　the letter?
VALENTINE
　　How now, sir? What, are you reasoning with yourself?
SPEED
130　Nay, I was rhyming. 'Tis you that have the reason.

VALENTINE
　　To do what?
SPEED
　　To be a spokesman from Madam Sylvia.
VALENTINE
　　To whom?
SPEED
　　To yourself. Why, she woos you by a figure.
VALENTINE
135　What figure?
SPEED
　　By a letter, I should say.
VALENTINE
　　Why, she hath not writ to me.

ACT 2, SCENE 1
NO FEAR SHAKESPEARE

SYLVIA
>And when it's written, read it over for my sake. And if it pleases you, fine. And if it doesn't, well, that's also fine.

VALENTINE
>If it pleases me, madame, what then?

SYLVIA
>Why, if it pleases you, then take it as payment for your hard work. And so good morning and goodbye to you, servant.
>
>>*SYLVIA exits.*

SPEED
>(*Aside*) Oh, that joke is as hard to see as a nose on a man's face or a weathercock on a steeple! My master pleads with her, and she has taught him, her student, to become her teacher. What an excellent trick! Has anyone ever heard anything better than my master, the scribe, writing the letter to himself?

VALENTINE
>What's that, sir? What are you reasoning to yourself over there?

SPEED
>No, I was rhyming. It's you who's been doing the reasoning.

VALENTINE
>Reasoning what?

SPEED
>To be a spokesman for Madame Sylvia.

VALENTINE
>To whom?

SPEED
>To yourself. Why, she's wooing you indirectly with this trick.

VALENTINE
>What trick?

SPEED
>By a letter, I should say.

VALENTINE
>But, she hasn't written to me.

Two Gentlemen of Verona   Act 2, Scen

SPEED
What need she, when she hath made you write to yourself? Why, do you not perceive the jest?

VALENTINE
140 No, believe me.

SPEED
No believing you, indeed, sir. But did you perceive her earnest?

VALENTINE
She gave me none, except an angry word.

SPEED
Why, she hath given you a letter.

VALENTINE
145 That's the letter I writ to her friend.

SPEED
And that letter hath she delivered, and there an end.

VALENTINE
I would it were no worse.

SPEED
I'll warrant you, 'tis as well.
For often have you writ to her, and she, in modesty,
150 Or else for want of idle time, could not again reply;
Or fearing else some messenger that might her
    mind discover,
Herself hath taught her love himself to write unto
    her lover.
155 All this I speak in print, for in print I found it. Why muse you, sir? 'Tis dinner time.

VALENTINE
I have dined.

SPEED
Ay, but hearken, sir: though the chameleon Love can feed on the air, I am one that am nourished by my victuals,
160 and would fain have meat. O, be not like your mistress; be moved, be moved!

Exeunt

ACT 2, SCENE 1
NO FEAR SHAKESPEARE

SPEED
> Why would she need to when she's made you write to yourself? Why, don't you get the joke?

VALENTINE
> No, believe me.

SPEED
> No believing you, indeed, sir. Did you think she was being serious?

VALENTINE
> She gave me nothing except an angry word.

SPEED
> Why, she's given you a letter.

VALENTINE
> That's the letter I wrote to her friend.

SPEED
> And she's delivered that letter, and that's the end of it.

VALENTINE
> I wish it were that good.

SPEED
> I promise you, it is that good. Because you've often written to her, and she, whether out of modesty or because she didn't have the time, or out of fear that the messenger carrying the letter would discover her feelings, couldn't reply. So she taught the man she loves to write to himself. I say all this very carefully, because I read it in her as if it were printed on a page. Why do you look so pensive, sir? It's lunchtime.

Chameleons were thought to feed on air since they can go long periods without eating. Here it also refers to love's fickleness, since chameleons can change their color.

VALENTINE
> I've already eaten.

SPEED
> Yes, but listen, sir: even though **the chameleon Love** can feed off the air, I need real food for nourishment and I'm eager to have meat. Oh, don't be like your mistress—have a heart!

They exit.

MODERN TEXT   53

ACT 2, SCENE 2

Enter PROTEUS *and* JULIA

PROTEUS
Have patience, gentle Julia.
JULIA
I must, where is no remedy.
PROTEUS
When possibly I can, I will return.
JULIA
If you turn not, you will return the sooner.
Keep this remembrance for thy Julia's sake.

(Giving a ring.)

PROTEUS
Why, then, we'll make exchange; here, take you this.

(He gives her a ring.)

JULIA
And seal the bargain with a holy kiss.

(They kiss.)

PROTEUS
Here is my hand for my true constancy;
And when that hour o'erslips me in the day
Wherein I sigh not, Julia, for thy sake,
The next ensuing hour some foul mischance
Torment me for my love's forgetfulness!
My father stays my coming. Answer not.
The tide is now—nay, not thy tide of tears;
That tide will stay me longer than I should.
Julia, farewell!

Exit JULIA

What, gone without a word?
Ay, so true love should do; it cannot speak,
For truth hath better deeds than words to grace it.

ACT 2, SCENE 2

PROTEUS *and* JULIA *enter.*

PROTEUS
Be patient, gentle Julia.

JULIA
I have to be, since there is no way to fix the situation.

PROTEUS
I will return as soon as I can.

JULIA
If you're not unfaithful you'll return sooner. Keep this to remember me by, for my sake.

(She gives him a ring.)

PROTEUS
Well, then, we'll exchange rings. Here, you take this.

(He gives her a ring.)

JULIA
And we will seal the bargain with a holy kiss.

(They kiss.)

PROTEUS
Here is my hand to show my fidelity. And if an hour in the day passes when I don't sigh when thinking of you, Julia, then may some disaster torment me in the next hour to punish my love's forgetfulness! My father is waiting for me. Don't say anything. The tide is right for me to set out—no, not your tide of tears. Those tears will keep me here longer than I should stay. Farewell, Julia!

JULIA *exits.*

What, she's gone without saying a word? Yes, that's how it should be with true love. It cannot speak, because truth is best expressed through action, not words.

Enter **PANTHINO**

PANTHINO
20   Sir Proteus, you are stayed for.
PROTEUS
      Go. I come, I come.
      Alas! This parting strikes poor lovers dumb.

Exeunt

ACT 2, SCENE 2
NO FEAR SHAKESPEARE

PANTHINO *enters.*

PANTHINO
Sir Proteus, everyone is waiting for you.

PROTEUS
Go on. I'm coming, I'm coming. Too bad! This parting has left us poor lovers without words.

They exit.

ACT 2, SCENE 3

Enter LAUNCE *(leading his dog, Crab)*

LAUNCE
Nay, 'twill be this hour ere I have done weeping. All the kind of the Launces have this very fault. I have received my proportion, like the prodigious son, and am going with Sir Proteus to the imperial's court. I think Crab, my dog, be the sourest-natured dog that lives. My mother weeping, my father wailing, my sister crying, our maid howling, our cat wringing her hands, and all our house in a great perplexity, yet did not this cruel-hearted cur shed one tear. He is a stone, a very pebblestone, and has no more pity in him than a dog. A Jew would have wept to have seen our parting. Why, my grandam, having no eyes, look you, wept herself blind at my parting. Nay, I'll show you the manner of it. This shoe is my father. No, this left shoe is my father. No, no, this left shoe is my mother. Nay, that cannot be so neither. Yes, it is so, it is so—it hath the worser sole. This shoe, with the hole in it, is my mother, and this my father. A vengeance on 't! There 'tis. Now, sir, this staff is my sister, for, look you, she is as white as a lily and as small as a wand. This hat is Nan, our maid. I am the dog. No, the dog is himself, and I am the dog—O! the dog is me, and I am myself. Ay, so, so. Now come I to my father: "Father, your blessing." Now should not the shoe speak a word for weeping. Now should I kiss my father. Well, he weeps on. Now come I to my mother. O, that she could speak now like a moved woman! Well, I kiss her. Why there 'tis. Here's my mother's breath up and down. Now come I to my sister; mark the moan she makes. Now the dog all this while sheds not a tear nor speaks a word; but see how I lay the dust with my tears.

ACT 2, SCENE 3

LAUNCE *enters, leading his dog, Crab.*

LAUNCE

No, it'll be this time tomorrow before I've stopped crying. All the members of the Launce family have this fault. I've received my portion of the family trait, just like the **prodigious son**, and now I'm going with Sir Proteus to the imperial court in Milan. I think Crab, my dog, has the sourest personality of any dog alive. Even with my mother weeping, my father wailing, my sister crying, our maid howling, and our cat wringing her hands, this cruel-hearted mutt didn't shed a single tear. **Even a Jewish person** would have wept to see us saying good-bye to each other. Why, my grandmother—who doesn't have use of her eyes, you see—cried herself blind when I said good-bye. No, I'll demonstrate what happened. This shoe represents my father. No, this left shoe is my father. No, no, this left shoe is my mother. No, that can't be right either. Yes it is, it is—it has the sole that isn't as good. This shoe, with the hole in it, is my mother, and this one is my father. Take that! That's right now. Now, sir, this wooden stick is my sister, because, you see, it is as white as a lily and as thin as a twig. This hat is Nan, our maid. I am the dog. No wait, the dog is himself, and I am the dog—oh, I mean, the dog is me, and I am myself. Okay, okay, that's it. Now I go to my father and say, "Father, give me your blessing." Now the shoe can't say a word because it's crying so hard. Now I'll kiss my father. Well, he keeps crying. Now I come to my mother. Oh, I wish this shoe could speak full of emotion now! Well, I kiss her. And that's the way it happened. Here's how she breathed from crying so

---

Launce, who frequently confuses words, means to refer to the biblical story of the Prodigal Son.

Shakespeare is casually negative about Jews, which comes up again later and in other plays. It has been debated whether Shakespeare had anti-Semitic views or was just exploring the negative sentiment prevalent in Europe at the time.

Two Gentlemen of Verona — Act 2, Scene 3

Enter PANTHINO

PANTHINO
Launce, away, away, aboard! Thy master is shipped, and thou art to post after with oars. What's the matter? Why weep'st thou, man? Away, ass! You'll lose the tide if you tarry any longer.

LAUNCE
It is no matter if the tied were lost; for it is the unkindest tied that ever any man tied.

PANTHINO
What's the unkindest tide?

LAUNCE
Why, he that's tied here, Crab, my dog.

PANTHINO
Tut, man, I mean thou'lt lose the flood, and in losing the flood, lose thy voyage, and in losing thy voyage, lose thy master, and, in losing thy master, lose thy service, and, in losing thy service—

(LAUNCE puts his hand over PANTHINO's mouth.)
Why dost thou stop my mouth?

LAUNCE
For fear thou shouldst lose thy tongue.

PANTHINO
Where should I lose my tongue?

LAUNCE
In thy tale.

PANTHINO
In thy tail!

much. Now I come to my sister. Listen to the moans she makes because she's so sad. All the while the dog doesn't shed a single tear or speak a word. See how I flatten the dust with my tears?

PANTHINO *enters.*

PANTHINO

Launce, go on, go on, board the ship! Your master is already aboard, and you're supposed to hurry after him in a rowboat. What's the matter? Why are you crying, man? Get on, you ass! You'll lose the tide if you delay any longer.

LAUNCE

It doesn't matter if this tied-up dog is lost, because it's the unkindest tied-up thing any man ever tied up.

PANTHINO

What's the unkindest tide?

LAUNCE

Why, the dog that's tied up right here—Crab, my dog.

PANTHINO

No, no, man, I mean you'll lose the ocean tide. And if you lose the ocean tide, then you'll lose the whole trip, and if you lose the whole trip, then you'll lose your master, and if you lose your master, then you'll lose your job, and if you lose your job . . .

(LAUNCE *puts his hand over* PANTHINO*'s mouth.*)
Why are you covering my mouth?

LAUNCE

Because I was afraid you'd lose your tongue.

PANTHINO

Where would I lose my tongue?

LAUNCE

In your tale.

PANTHINO

Up *your* tail!

LAUNCE
>Lose the tide, and the voyage, and the master, and the service, and the tied! Why, man, if the river were dry, I am able to fill it with my tears; if the wind were down, I could drive the boat with my sighs.

PANTHINO
>Come, come away, man. I was sent to call thee.

LAUNCE
>Sir, call me what thou darest.

PANTHINO
>Will thou go?

LAUNCE
>Well, I will go.

Exeunt.

ACT 2, SCENE 3
NO FEAR SHAKESPEARE

LAUNCE
> Lose the tide, and the voyage, and my master, and my job, and the tied-up dog! Why, man, if the river where the ship is moored dried up, I'd be able to fill it with my tears. And if the wind weren't blowing, I could blow the boat forward with my sighs.

PANTHINO
> Come on, come on, man. I was sent here to get you.

LAUNCE
> Sir, you can call me whatever you like.

PANTHINO
> Well, are you going to go?

LAUNCE
> Yes, I'll go.

They exit.

ACT 2, SCENE 4

Enter VALENTINE, SYLVIA, THURIO, *and* SPEED

SYLVIA
Servant!
VALENTINE
Mistress?
SPEED
Master, Sir Thurio frowns on you.
VALENTINE
Ay, boy, it's for love.
SPEED
5   Not of you.
VALENTINE
Of my mistress, then.
SPEED
'Twere good you knocked him.

Exit SPEED

SYLVIA
Servant, you are sad.
VALENTINE
Indeed, madam, I seem so.
THURIO
10 Seem you that you are not?
VALENTINE
Haply I do.
THURIO
So do counterfeits.
VALENTINE
So do you.
THURIO
What seem I that I am not?
VALENTINE
15 Wise.

ACT 2, SCENE 4

VALENTINE, SYLVIA, THURIO, *and* SPEED *enter*.

SYLVIA
Servant!

VALENTINE
Mistress?

SPEED
Master, Sir Thurio is frowning at you.

VALENTINE
Yes, boy, it's because he's in love.

SPEED
Not with you.

VALENTINE
With my mistress, then.

SPEED
It would be good if you punched him.

SPEED exits.

SYLVIA
Servant, you are sad.

VALENTINE
Indeed, madame, I seem to be.

THURIO
It seems you're sad when you are not?

VALENTINE
As it happens, I seem to be something I'm not.

THURIO
Just like a fake.

VALENTINE
You also seem to be something you're not.

THURIO
What do I seem like that I am not?

VALENTINE
Wise.

THURIO
    What instance of the contrary?
VALENTINE
    Your folly.
THURIO
    And how quote you my folly?
VALENTINE
    I quote it in your jerkin.
THURIO
    My "jerkin" is a doublet.
VALENTINE
    Well, then, I'll double your folly.
THURIO
    How?
SYLVIA
    What, angry, Sir Thurio? Do you change color?

VALENTINE
    Give him leave, madam; he is a kind of chameleon.
THURIO
    That hath more mind to feed on your blood than live in your air.
VALENTINE
    You have said, sir.
THURIO
    Ay, sir, and done too, for this time.
VALENTINE
    I know it well, sir; you always end ere you begin.
SYLVIA
    A fine volley of words, gentlemen, and quickly shot off.
VALENTINE
    'Tis indeed, madam, we thank the giver.
SYLVIA
    Who is that, servant?

ACT 2, SCENE 4
NO FEAR SHAKESPEARE

THURIO
What proof do you have to the contrary?

VALENTINE
Your foolishness.

THURIO
And what do you know of my foolishness?

VALENTINE
Because you're wearing a **jerkin**. — *A short coat.*

THURIO
My "jerkin" is actually a **doublet**. — *A jacket.*

VALENTINE
Well, then, you're doubly foolish.

THURIO
Why?

SYLVIA
What, are you angry, Sir Thurio? Is your face turning red?

VALENTINE
Leave him be, madame. He's just a kind of chameleon.

THURIO
One that would rather feed off your blood, Valentine, than its usual diet of air.

VALENTINE
So you say, sir.

THURIO
Yes, sir, and it'll be done, too.

VALENTINE
I know it's done, sir. You always end before you begin.

SYLVIA
A fine volley of words, gentlemen, and quickly fired.

VALENTINE
It is indeed, madame. We have the giver to thank for that.

SYLVIA
And who is the giver, servant?

MODERN TEXT

VALENTINE
>Yourself, sweet lady, for you gave the fire. Sir Thurio
>borrows his wit from your ladyship's looks, and spends
>what he borrows kindly in your company.

THURIO
>Sir, if you spend word for word with me, I shall make
>your wit bankrupt.

VALENTINE
>I know it well, sir; you have an exchequer of words, and,
>I think, no other treasure to give your followers, for it
>appears, by their bare liveries, that they live by your
>bare words.

SYLVIA
>No more, gentlemen, no more. Here comes my father.

Enter the DUKE.

DUKE
>Now, daughter Sylvia, you are hard beset.
>Sir Valentine, your father is in good health.
>What say you to a letter from your friends
>Of much good news?

VALENTINE
>My lord, I will be thankful
>To any happy messenger from thence.

DUKE
>Know ye Don Antonio, your countryman?

VALENTINE
>Ay, my good lord, I know the gentleman
>To be of worth and worthy estimation,
>And not without desert so well reputed.

DUKE
>Hath he not a son?

VALENTINE
>Ay, my good lord, a son that well deserves
>The honor and regard of such a father.

ACT 2, SCENE 4
NO FEAR SHAKESPEARE

VALENTINE

> Yourself, sweet lady, for you provided the spark that set it off. Sir Thurio gets his witty remarks from your ladyship's good looks, and he appropriately spends what he borrows in your presence.

THURIO

> Sir, if you spar word for word with me, I shall make your wit dry up.

VALENTINE

> I know it well, sir. You have a whole treasury of words, and, I think, no other treasure to give your servants, since it appears, by their ragged clothing, that they live by your worthless words alone.

SYLVIA

> No more, gentlemen, no more. Here comes my father.

> *The DUKE enters.*

DUKE

> Now, my daughter Sylvia, you are being assaulted. Sir Valentine, your father is healthy. What would you say to a letter from your friends filled with good news?

VALENTINE

> My lord, I would be thankful to anyone who brought good news from home.

DUKE

> Do you know Don Antonio, who is also from your country?

VALENTINE

> Yes, my good lord. I know the gentleman is noble and has a good reputation, which is well deserved.

DUKE

> Doesn't he have a son?

VALENTINE

> Yes, my good lord, a son that is also deserving of the honor and reputation of his esteemed father.

DUKE
You know him well?

VALENTINE
I knew him as myself, for from our infancy
We have conversed and spent our hours together.
And though myself have been an idle truant,
Omitting the sweet benefit of time
To clothe mine age with angel-like perfection,
Yet hath Sir Proteus—for that's his name—
Made use and fair advantage of his days;
His years but young, but his experience old;
His head unmellowed, but his judgment ripe.
And, in a word—for far behind his worth
Comes all the praises that I now bestow—
He is complete in feature and in mind
With all good grace to grace a gentleman.

DUKE
Beshrew me, sir, but if he make this good,
He is as worthy for an empress' love
As meet to be an emperor's counselor.
Well, sir, this gentleman is come to me,
With commendation from great potentates,
And here he means to spend his time awhile.
I think 'tis no unwelcome news to you.

VALENTINE
Should I have wished a thing, it had been he.

DUKE
Welcome him then according to his worth.
Sylvia, I speak to you, and you, Sir Thurio;
For Valentine, I need not cite him to it.
I will send him hither to you presently.

Exit the **DUKE**

VALENTINE
This is the gentleman I told your ladyship
Had come along with me but that his mistress
Did hold his eyes locked in her crystal looks.

ACT 2, SCENE 4
NO FEAR SHAKESPEARE

DUKE
> Do you know him well?

VALENTINE
> I know him as well as I know myself, since he and I have been in each other's company and spent time together since we were infants. And even though I myself have been an unproductive delinquent and have wasted my youth on frivolity, Sir Proteus—that's his name, you see—made good use of his time. He may be young, but he has the experience of a much older person. His hair isn't gray, but his judgment is wise. Any praise I give is far less than he deserves, but in a word, he is perfect physically and mentally, with all the good graces of a true gentleman.

DUKE
> Damn! Sir, if this account is true, he is as worthy of an empress's love as he is fit to be an emperor's adviser. Well, sir, this gentleman has come to me with commendations from powerful men, and he intends to spend his time here for a while. I think it's good news for you.

VALENTINE
> If I had wished for anything, it would have been for him to come.

DUKE
> Then give him the welcome he deserves. I'm speaking to you, Sylvia, and you, Sir Thurio. Valentine needs no urging. I will send him to you here shortly.
>
> *The* DUKE *exits.*

VALENTINE
> This is the gentleman I told your ladyship would have come along with me had the woman he loved not captivated him with her beauty.

SYLVIA
Belike that now she hath enfranchised them
Upon some other pawn for fealty.
VALENTINE
Nay, sure, I think she holds them prisoners still.
SYLVIA
Nay, then he should be blind, and being blind
How could he see his way to seek out you?
VALENTINE
Why, lady, Love hath twenty pair of eyes.
THURIO
They say that Love hath not an eye at all.
VALENTINE
To see such lovers, Thurio, as yourself.
Upon a homely object Love can wink.
SYLVIA
Have done, have done. Here comes the gentleman.

Enter PROTEUS.

VALENTINE
Welcome, dear Proteus!—Mistress, I beseech you,
Confirm his welcome with some special favor.
SYLVIA
His worth is warrant for his welcome hither,
If this be he you oft have wished to hear from.
VALENTINE
Mistress, it is. Sweet lady, entertain him
To be my fellow servant to your ladyship.
SYLVIA
Too low a mistress for so high a servant.
PROTEUS
Not so, sweet lady, but too mean a servant
To have a look of such a worthy mistress.

ACT 2, SCENE 4
NO FEAR SHAKESPEARE

SYLVIA
> Perhaps now she's freed him because some other lover has pledged devotion to her.

VALENTINE
> No, I'm sure she still holds him prisoner.

SYLVIA
> No, if that were true, then he would be blind, and if he were blind, how could he see to find his way to you?

VALENTINE
> Why, lady, Love has twenty pairs of eyes.

THURIO
> They say that Love is blind and has no eyes at all.

VALENTINE
> Love has no eyes for people like you, Thurio. Love can shut its eyes to ugly things.

SYLVIA
> Stop, stop. Here comes the gentleman.

PROTEUS enters.

VALENTINE
> Welcome, dear Proteus! Mistress, I beg you, make him feel welcome by giving him some sign of your affection.

SYLVIA
> His worthiness is enough for us to welcome here if he's the one you've often wished to hear from.

VALENTINE
> Mistress, it is he. Sweet lady, take him into your service to be my fellow servant to your ladyship.

SYLVIA
> I'm too unworthy a mistress for so noble a servant.

PROTEUS
> Not so, sweet lady. I'm too unworthy a servant to have caught a look from a worthy mistress.

VALENTINE
Leave off discourse of disability.
105 Sweet lady, entertain him for your servant.

PROTEUS
My duty will I boast of, nothing else.

SYLVIA
And duty never yet did want his meed.
Servant, you are welcome to a worthless mistress.

PROTEUS
I'll die on him that says so but yourself.

SYLVIA
110 That you are welcome?

PROTEUS
That you are worthless.

Enter a SERVANT.

SERVANT
Madam, my lord your father would speak with you.

SYLVIA
I wait upon his pleasure.

Exit SERVANT

Come, Sir Thurio,
115 Go with me. Once more, new servant, welcome.
I'll leave you to confer of home affairs.
When you have done we look to hear from you.

PROTEUS
We'll both attend upon your ladyship.

Exeunt SYLVIA *and* THURIO

VALENTINE
Now tell me, how do all from whence you came?

PROTEUS
120 Your friends are well and have them much commended.

ACT 2, SCENE 4
NO FEAR SHAKESPEARE

VALENTINE
> Don't talk about unworthiness. Sweet lady, ask him to be your servant.

PROTEUS
> I'll only boast of my duty, nothing else.

SYLVIA
> And duty never did go unrewarded. Servant, I, a worthless mistress, welcome you.

PROTEUS
> I'll die fighting anyone who says that but you.

SYLVIA
> That you are welcome?

PROTEUS
> That you are worthless.

A **SERVANT** *enters.*

SERVANT
> Madame, my lord—your father—would like to speak with you.

SYLVIA
> I'll be there in a moment.
>
> *The* **SERVANT** *exits.*
>
> Come, Sir Thurio, go with me. Again, I welcome you, new servant. I'll leave you to talk with your friend about affairs back home. We look forward to seeing you when you're finished.

PROTEUS
> We'll both be back to serve you shortly, your ladyship.
>
> **SYLVIA** *and* **THURIO** *exit.*

VALENTINE
> Now tell me, how is everyone back home?

PROTEUS
> Your friends are well and send their regards.

VALENTINE
    And how do yours?
PROTEUS
                I left them all in health.
VALENTINE
    How does your lady, and how thrives your love?
PROTEUS
    My tales of love were wont to weary you;
125   I know you joy not in a love discourse.
VALENTINE
    Ay, Proteus, but that life is altered now.
    I have done penance for contemning Love,
    Whose high imperious thoughts have punished me
    With bitter fasts, with penitential groans,
130   With nightly tears, and daily heartsore sighs;
    For, in revenge of my contempt of love,
    Love hath chased sleep from my enthrallèd eyes
    And made them watchers of mine own heart's sorrow.
    O gentle Proteus, Love's a mighty lord,
135   And hath so humbled me as I confess
    There is no woe to his correction,
    Nor to his service no such joy on earth.
    Now, no discourse, except it be of love;
    Now can I break my fast, dine, sup, and sleep
140   Upon the very naked name of love.
PROTEUS
    Enough. I read your fortune in your eye.
    Was this the idol that you worship so?
VALENTINE
    Even she. And is she not a heavenly saint?
PROTEUS
    No, but she is an earthly paragon.
VALENTINE
145   Call her divine.
PROTEUS
                I will not flatter her.

ACT 2, SCENE 4
NO FEAR SHAKESPEARE

VALENTINE
And how are your friends?

PROTEUS
They were all fine and healthy when I left.

VALENTINE
How is your lady, and is your love thriving?

PROTEUS
My tales of love used to bore you. I know you don't enjoy talking about love.

VALENTINE
Yes, Proteus, but my life is different now. I have atoned for condemning Love. Overbearing thoughts of love punish me with bitter periods of not eating, remorseful groans, nightly tears, and daily lovesick sighs. In revenge for my contempt, Love keeps me awake and makes my eyes watch the woman responsible for my heart's sorrow. Oh, kind Proteus, Love's a powerful ruler and has so humbled me that I confess there is no sorrow as bad as his punishment and no joy equal to being in love. Now, speak no more unless it's about love. Now I can eat again, have lunch and dinner, and sleep thinking of love.

PROTEUS
Enough. I knew how you felt from the look in your eyes. Was that the woman you worship like an idol?

VALENTINE
That was she. Isn't she a heavenly saint?

PROTEUS
No, but she is a model of beauty here on earth.

VALENTINE
Call her a goddess.

PROTEUS
I will not fawn over her.

MODERN TEXT

Two Gentlemen of Verona — Act 2, Scene 4

VALENTINE
    O, flatter me, for love delights in praises.

PROTEUS
    When I was sick, you gave me bitter pills,
    And I must minister the like to you.

VALENTINE
150   Then speak the truth by her; if not divine,
    Yet let her be a principality,
    Sovereign to all the creatures on the earth.

PROTEUS
    Except my mistress.

VALENTINE
                   Sweet, except not any,
155   Except thou wilt except against my love.

PROTEUS
    Have I not reason to prefer mine own?

VALENTINE
    And I will help thee to prefer her, too.
    She shall be dignified with this high honor:
    To bear my lady's train, lest the base earth
160   Should from her vesture chance to steal a kiss
    And, of so great a favor growing proud,
    Disdain to root the summer-swelling flower
    And make rough winter everlastingly.

PROTEUS
    Why, Valentine, what braggartism is this?

VALENTINE
165   Pardon me, Proteus, all I can is nothing
    To her whose worth makes other worthies nothing.
    She is alone.

PROTEUS
    Then, let her alone.

VALENTINE
    Not for the world. Why, man, she is mine own,
170   And I as rich in having such a jewel

ACT 2, SCENE 4
NO FEAR SHAKESPEARE

VALENTINE
> Oh, flatter me, then, because those who are in love delight in praise.

PROTEUS
> When I was lovesick, you gave me the hard truth, and now I must give it to you.

VALENTINE
> Then speak the truth about her. If she isn't a goddess, then call her an angel who is superior to all the creatures on earth.

PROTEUS
> Except my mistress.

VALENTINE
> No exceptions, my friend, unless you mean to insult my love.

PROTEUS
> Don't I have reason to put forward my own girl?

VALENTINE
> And I will help you to put her forward, too. She shall have the dignity of having this high honor: she can carry the train of my lady's dress so that the dirty ground can't steal a kiss of her clothing. If it did, the ground would swell so much with pride that it would no longer accept the roots of the summer flowers, and rough winter would last forever.

PROTEUS
> Geez, Valentine, why are you bragging so much?

VALENTINE
> Pardon me, Proteus, any praise I can give is nothing in comparison with her. She is unique and alone among women.

PROTEUS
> Then leave her alone.

VALENTINE
> Not for the world. Why, man, she is mine, and having a jewel such as her, I'm as rich as if I had twenty oceans

          As twenty seas, if all their sand were pearl,
          The water nectar, and the rocks pure gold.
          Forgive me that I do not dream on thee,
          Because thou seest me dote upon my love.
175   My foolish rival, that her father likes
          Only for his possessions are so huge,
          Is gone with her along, and I must after,
          For love, thou know'st, is full of jealousy.

PROTEUS
          But she loves you?

VALENTINE
180   Ay, and we are betrothed. Nay, more, our marriage-hour,
          With all the cunning manner of our flight,
          Determined of—how I must climb her window,
          The ladder made of cords, and all the means
          Plotted and 'greed on for my happiness.
185   Good Proteus, go with me to my chamber,
          In these affairs to aid me with thy counsel.

PROTEUS
          Go on before; I shall enquire you forth.
          I must unto the road, to disembark
          Some necessaries that I needs must use,
190   And then I'll presently attend you.

VALENTINE
          Will you make haste?

                                              Exit **VALENTINE**

PROTEUS
          I will.
          Even as one heat another heat expels,
          Or as one nail by strength drives out another,
195   So the remembrance of my former love
          Is by a newer object quite forgotten.
          Is it my mind, or Valentine's praise,
          Her true perfection, or my false transgression
          That makes me, reasonless, to reason thus?

with sands made of pearls, water of nectar, and rocks of pure gold. Forgive me for not paying attention to you, because I'm doting on the woman I love, as you can tell. Her father likes my foolish rival, Thurio, because he has so much wealth. Thurio has gone with her, and I must follow after them, because love, as you know, is prone to jealousy.

PROTEUS

But does she love you?

VALENTINE

Yes, and we're engaged to be married. No, what's more, we've determined all the details of how we'll sneak away and elope—how I must climb up to her window on a ladder made of rope. Everything is arranged and agreed upon for my happiness. Good Proteus, go with me to my bedroom to give me some advice on these matters.

PROTEUS

Go on ahead. I'll find you shortly. I must go down to the harbor to bring ashore some necessities that I need. Then I'll come see you right away.

VALENTINE

Will you hurry?

VALENTINE exits.

PROTEUS

I will. Just as **one heat can extinguish another**, or as one nail can drive another out with force, so too has a new love, Sylvia, driven out the memory of my former love, Julia. Is it my own attraction for her, or Valentine's praise, or her own perfection, or going against my love for Julia that makes me feel this way? She is beautiful, but so is Julia, whom I love— whom I did love, because now my love for her has

At the time, it was believed that applying heat on a burn would take away the pain.

She is fair; and so is Julia that I love—
That I did love, for now my love is thawed,
Which like a waxen image 'gainst a fire
Bears no impression of the thing it was.
Methinks my zeal to Valentine is cold,
And that I love him not as I was wont.
O, but I love his lady too, too much,
And that's the reason I love him so little.
How shall I dote on her with more advice,
That thus without advice begin to love her!
'Tis but her picture I have yet beheld,
And that hath dazzlèd my reason's light;
But when I look on her perfections,
There is no reason but I shall be blind.
If I can check my erring love, I will;
If not, to compass her I'll use my skill.

Exit

ACT 2, SCENE 4
NO FEAR SHAKESPEARE

melted away, like a wax figure melted by a fire that no longer looks as it did. I think that my fondness for Valentine has diminished, too, and that I like him less than I used to. Oh, but I love his lady, Sylvia, far too much, and that's why I like him less now. How can I keep from loving her after further deliberation when I begin to love her with no deliberation at all! It's only her surface I've seen so far, and that has already confused my sense of reason. But when I look at her perfection, there is no doubt I will be blind with love. If I can stop my love, I will. If not, I'll use my skill to win her.

He exits.

ACT 2, SCENE 5

Enter, (meeting,) SPEED *and* LAUNCE *(with his dog, Crab)*

SPEED
Launce, by mine honesty, welcome to Milan!

LAUNCE
Forswear not thyself, sweet youth, for I am not welcome.
I reckon this always, that a man is never undone till he
be hanged, nor never welcome to a place till some certain
shot be paid and the hostess say "Welcome!"

SPEED
Come on, you madcap, I'll to the alehouse with you
presently, where, for one shot of five pence, thou shalt
have five thousand welcomes. But, sirrah, how did thy
master part with Madam Julia?

LAUNCE
Marry, after they closed in earnest, they parted very fairly
in jest.

SPEED
But shall she marry him?

LAUNCE
No.

SPEED
How then? Shall he marry her?

LAUNCE
No, neither.

SPEED
What, are they broken?

LAUNCE
No, they are both as whole as a fish.

SPEED
Why, then, how stands the matter with them?

LAUNCE
Marry, thus: when it stands well with him, it stands well
with her.

ACT 2, SCENE 5

SPEED *and* LAUNCE, *with his dog, Crab, enter and meet.*

SPEED

Launce, honestly, welcome to Milan!

LAUNCE

Don't lie, my friend, because I am not welcome. I always believe a man is never sunk until he's hanged, nor ever welcome to a place until the bill has been paid and the hostess says, "Welcome!"

SPEED

Come you, you lunatic, I'll go to the pub with you soon, where you can have five thousand welcomes for five pence. But tell me, pal, how did your master say good-bye to Madame Julia?

LAUNCE

You know, after they said their earnest good-byes, they parted with a few jokes.

SPEED

But will she marry him?

LAUNCE

No.

SPEED

What then? Will he marry her?

LAUNCE

No, not that either.

SPEED

What, have they broken up?

LAUNCE

No, they're as whole as ever.

SPEED

Well, then, where do they stand on the matter?

LAUNCE

Indeed, that's the way it is: when he stands erect, he's in good standing with her.

SPEED
> What an ass art thou! I understand thee not.

LAUNCE
> What a block art thou, that thou canst not! My staff understands me.

SPEED
> What thou sayest?

LAUNCE
> Ay, and what I do too. Look thee, I'll but lean, and my staff understands me.

SPEED
> It stands under thee, indeed.

LAUNCE
> Why, stand-under and under-stand is all one.

SPEED
> But tell me true, will 't be a match?

LAUNCE
> Ask my dog. If he say ay, it will; if he say no, it will; if he shake his tail and say nothing, it will.

SPEED
> The conclusion is then that it will.

LAUNCE
> Thou shalt never get such a secret from me but by a parable.

SPEED
> 'Tis well that I get it so. But, Launce, how sayest thou, that my master is become a notable lover?

LAUNCE
> I never knew him otherwise.

SPEED
> Than how?

LAUNCE
> A notable lubber, as thou reportest him to be.

ACT 2, SCENE 5
NO FEAR SHAKESPEARE

SPEED

What an ass you are! I don't understand you.

LAUNCE

What a blockhead you are, since you can't understand me! My wooden staff understands me.

SPEED

What are you talking about?

LAUNCE

Yes, and it's what I do, too. Look here—I simply have to lean, and my staff understands me.

SPEED

It stands under you, indeed.

LAUNCE

Well, standing-under, under-standing—it's all the same.

SPEED

But tell me honestly, will they get married?

LAUNCE

Ask my dog. If he says yes, then they will. If he says no, then they will. If he shakes his tail and says nothing, then they will.

SPEED

So no matter what then, they will get married.

LAUNCE

You'll never get me to reveal the secret except in riddles.

SPEED

It's best that I find out that way. But, Launce, what can you tell me about the fact that my master has become a well-known lover?

LAUNCE

I never knew him otherwise.

SPEED

Than what?

LAUNCE

A well-known **lubber**—and idiot, as you've told me he is.

A big, clumsy oaf.

SPEED
Why, thou whoreson ass, thou mistakest me.

LAUNCE
Why, fool, I meant not thee. I meant thy master.

SPEED
I tell thee, my master is become a hot lover.

LAUNCE
Why, I tell thee I care not, though he burn himself in love. If thou wilt, go with me to the alehouse; if not, thou art an Hebrew, a Jew, and not worth the name of a Christian.

SPEED
Why?

LAUNCE
Because thou hast not so much charity in thee as to go to the ale with a Christian. Wilt thou go?

SPEED
At thy service.

Exeunt

ACT 2, SCENE 5
NO FEAR SHAKESPEARE

SPEED

> Why, you jackass **son of a whore**! You misunderstand me.

This term was often used jokingly.

LAUNCE

> Why, fool, I didn't mean you. I meant your master.

SPEED

> I tell you, my master has become an excellent lover.

LAUNCE

> Well, I tell you that I don't really care, even if he burns himself from being so "hot" in love. Come with me to the pub if you will. If not, then you're **a Hebrew, a Jew**, and not worthy to be called a Christian.

Again here in this text Shakespeare makes a casually negative remark about Jews.

SPEED

> Why?

LAUNCE

> Because you don't even have enough compassion in you to go to **the church's ale festival** with a Christian. So, are you coming?

SPEED

> I'm at your service.

They exit.

A charitable festival in which ale was sold and the proceeds helped the church or went to the poor.

MODERN TEXT

ACT 2, SCENE 6

Enter PROTEUS *solus*

PROTEUS
>To leave my Julia, shall I be forsworn;
>To love fair Sylvia, shall I be forsworn;
>To wrong my friend, I shall be much forsworn.
>And ev'n that power which gave me first my oath
>Provokes me to this threefold perjury.
>Love bade me swear, and Love bids me forswear.
>O sweet-suggesting Love, if thou hast sinned,
>Teach me, thy tempted subject, to excuse it!
>At first I did adore a twinkling star,
>But now I worship a celestial sun.
>Unheedful vows may heedfully be broken,
>And he wants wit that wants resolvèd will
>To learn his wit t' exchange the bad for better.
>Fie, fie, unreverent tongue, to call her bad
>Whose sovereignty so oft thou hast preferred
>With twenty thousand soul-confirming oaths!
>I cannot leave to love, and yet I do;
>But there I leave to love where I should love.
>Julia I lose, and Valentine I lose.
>If I keep them, I needs must lose myself.
>If I lose them, thus find I by their loss
>For Valentine, myself; for Julia, Sylvia.
>I to myself am dearer than a friend,
>For love is still most precious in itself,
>And Sylvia—witness heaven, that made her fair!—
>Shows Julia but a swarthy Ethiop.
>I will forget that Julia is alive,
>Remembering that my love to her is dead;
>And Valentine I'll hold an enemy,
>Aiming at Sylvia as a sweeter friend.
>I cannot now prove constant to myself

ACT 2, SCENE 6

PROTEUS *enters by himself.*

PROTEUS

If I leave my Julia, I'll break my vow and prove it a lie. If I love the beautiful Sylvia, I'll break my vow. If I wrong my friend, Valentine, I'll very much break my vow. And even that love that made me first declare my devotion provokes me to break my vow three times over. Love made me swear an oath, and love bids me to break it. Oh, sweet, seductive Love, if you have sinned, teach me, your tempted servant, how to pardon that sin. At first, I adored a twinkling star, but now I worship a heavenly sun. Vows made carelessly may be broken with careful thought, and the man who doesn't have the will to teach his mind to trade something bad for something better lacks intelligence. Shame, shame! What a disrespectful tongue I have to call Julia bad, when my tongue has so often praised her superiority with twenty thousand devout oaths of love! I cannot stop loving her, and yet I do. But in ceasing to love her I go to the woman I should love. I lose Julia, and I lose Valentine. If I keep them, then I will lose myself. If I lose them, then I'll gain myself instead of Valentine, and I'll gain Sylvia instead of Julia. I cherish myself more than I cherish any friend, for love of oneself is always most precious. And Sylvia—with heaven, which made her white and beautiful, as witness—makes Julia look like a **dark-skinned Ethiopian**. I will forget that Julia is alive, and remember that my love for her is gone. I'll consider Valentine an enemy and focus on Sylvia as a more important friend. I cannot now keep my promise to myself without acting treacherously toward

Fair skin was part of the European ideal of beauty.

Without some treachery used to Valentine.
This night he meaneth with a corded ladder
To climb celestial Sylvia's chamber window,
Myself in counsel, his competitor.
Now presently I'll give her father notice
Of their disguising and pretended flight,
Who, all enraged, will banish Valentine;
For Thurio, he intends, shall wed his daughter;
But, Valentine being gone, I'll quickly cross
By some sly trick blunt Thurio's dull proceeding.
Love, lend me wings to make my purpose swift,
As thou hast lent me wit to plot this drift!

Exit

ACT 2, SCENE 6
NO FEAR SHAKESPEARE

Valentine. Tonight he plans to climb a rope ladder to the heavenly Sylvia's bedroom window with me helping as his partner. Now I'll go immediately and inform her father of their secret and their plan to run away. He will be enraged and will banish Valentine, because he intends Thurio to marry his daughter. With Valentine gone, I'll ruin stupid Thurio's plans with some sly trick. Love, lend me wings so that I may accomplish my aims quickly, as you've lent me cleverness to plot this scheme!

He exits.

ACT 2, SCENE 7

Enter JULIA *and* LUCETTA

JULIA
Counsel, Lucetta. Gentle girl, assist me;
And ev'n in kind love I do conjure thee,
Who art the table wherein all my thoughts
Are visibly charactered and engraved,
To lesson me and tell me some good means
How, with my honor, I may undertake
A journey to my loving Proteus.

LUCETTA
Alas, the way is wearisome and long!

JULIA
A true-devoted pilgrim is not weary
To measure kingdoms with his feeble steps;
Much less shall she that hath Love's wings to fly,
And when the flight is made to one so dear,
Of such divine perfection, as Sir Proteus.

LUCETTA
Better forbear till Proteus make return.

JULIA
O! know'st thou not his looks are my soul's food?
Pity the dearth that I have pinèd in
By longing for that food so long a time.
Didst thou but know the inly touch of love,
Thou wouldst as soon go kindle fire with snow
As seek to quench the fire of love with words.

LUCETTA
I do not seek to quench your love's hot fire,
But qualify the fire's extreme rage,
Lest it should burn above the bounds of reason.

JULIA
The more thou damm'st it up, the more it burns.
The current that with gentle murmur glides,

ACT 2, SCENE 7

JULIA *and* LUCETTA *enter.*

JULIA

> I need your advice, Lucetta. Gentle girl, help me. And even in kind love I ask you to help me. You are my drawing board where all my thoughts can be visibly laid out and arranged. Teach me and tell me a good way I can make a journey to my loving Proteus with my honor intact.

LUCETTA

> Unfortunately, the way is exhausting and long!

JULIA

> A truly devoted traveler doesn't fear crossing entire kingdoms with small steps. She who has Love's wings to help her fly will get much less tired, especially when she makes the flight to one so dear and of such divine perfection as Sir Proteus.

LUCETTA

> It would be better if you waited until Proteus returned.

JULIA

> Oh, don't you know that his looks are food for my soul? Pity the famine I've endured by being without that food for so long. If you only knew the inner touch of love, you would as soon try to start a fire with snow as you would try to snuff the love's fire with words.

LUCETTA

> I do not seek to snuff your love's hot fire but merely want to reduce the intensity of the fire so that it doesn't burn out of your control.

JULIA

> The more you try to smother the fire, the more it burns. A gentle current of water will rage turbulently

Thou know'st, being stopped, impatiently doth rage;
But when his fair course is not hinderèd,
He makes sweet music with th' enameled stones,
Giving a gentle kiss to every sedge
30 He overtaketh in his pilgrimage,
And so by many winding nooks he strays
With willing sport to the wild ocean.
Then let me go, and hinder not my course.
I'll be as patient as a gentle stream
35 And make a pastime of each weary step,
Till the last step have brought me to my love,
And there I'll rest, as after much turmoil
A blessèd soul doth in Elysium.

LUCETTA
But in what habit will you go along?

JULIA
40 Not like a woman, for I would prevent
The loose encounters of lascivious men.
Gentle Lucetta, fit me with such weeds
As may beseem some well-reputed page.

LUCETTA
Why, then, your ladyship must cut your hair.

JULIA
45 No, girl, I'll knit it up in silken strings
With twenty odd-conceited true-love knots.
To be fantastic may become a youth
Of greater time than I shall show to be.

LUCETTA
What fashion, madam, shall I make your breeches?

JULIA
50 That fits as well as "Tell me, good my lord,
What compass will you wear your farthingale?"
Why, even what fashion thou best likes, Lucetta.

LUCETTA
You must needs have them with a codpiece, madam.

if blocked, you know. But when the current isn't hindered, it makes a sweet noise over the smooth, shiny stones, giving a gentle kiss to every blade of sedge grass that it passes over on its journey. And so it wanders past many curvy nooks as it heads playfully to the wild ocean. So let me go, and don't hinder my course. I'll be as patient as a gentle stream and enjoy each tiring step, until the last step has brought me to my love. There I'll rest, just like a blessed soul rests in **Elysium** after a tumultuous life.

The paradise of Greek mythology.

LUCETTA

But what clothing will you wear on your journey?

JULIA

I won't dress like a woman so that I can prevent the shameless sexual advances of lustful men. Kind Lucetta, outfit me with clothing appropriate for a young man from a good family.

LUCETTA

Well, then, your ladyship must cut your hair.

JULIA

No, girl, I'll tie it up in strange knots with silk ribbons. Fancy frills would look more appropriate on a young man who is slightly older than I'll appear to be.

LUCETTA

In what style, madame, should I make your pants?

JULIA

Any style that won't make men ask, "Tell me, good lord, how big around is the hoop in your hoop skirt?" Why, you should make them in whatever style you like best, Lucetta.

LUCETTA

You'll need to wear a cup in your crotch, madame.

JULIA
    Out, out, Lucetta! That will be ill-favored.
LUCETTA
    A round hose, madam, now's not worth a pin
    Unless you have a codpiece to stick pins on.
JULIA
    Lucetta, as thou lov'st me, let me have
    What thou think'st meet and is most mannerly.
    But tell me, wench, how will the world repute me
    For undertaking so unstaid a journey?
    I fear me it will make me scandalized.
LUCETTA
    If you think so, then stay at home and go not.
JULIA
    Nay, that I will not.
LUCETTA
    Then never dream on infamy, but go.
    If Proteus like your journey when you come,
    No matter who's displeased when you are gone.
    I fear me he will scarce be pleased withal.
JULIA
    That is the least, Lucetta, of my fear.
    A thousand oaths, an ocean of his tears,
    And instances of infinite of love,
    Warrant me welcome to my Proteus.
LUCETTA
    All these are servants to deceitful men.
JULIA
    Base men that use them to so base effect!
    But truer stars did govern Proteus' birth;
    His words are bonds, his oaths are oracles,
    His love sincere, his thoughts immaculate,
    His tears pure messengers sent from his heart,
    His heart as far from fraud as heaven from earth.
LUCETTA
    Pray heaven he prove so when you come to him!

NO FEAR SHAKESPEARE
ACT 2, SCENE 7

JULIA

Not so, Lucetta! That would be ugly.

LUCETTA

Tight leggings, madame, won't be much of a disguise unless you wear a cup.

JULIA

Lucetta, if you love me, let me have whatever you think is the most appropriate and fitting. But tell me, girl, what will people think of me for going on such a risky journey? I'm afraid it would make others think less of me.

LUCETTA

If that's what you think, then stay home and don't go.

JULIA

No, I won't stay.

LUCETTA

Then go, and don't worry what others might say. If Proteus is happy with your journey it doesn't matter who's displeased when they find out you've left. I'm afraid, though, that he won't be pleased.

JULIA

That is the least of my fears, Lucetta. A thousand oaths, an ocean of tears he cried, and many examples of his infinite love for me guarantee that Proteus will welcome me.

LUCETTA

These are the tricks of deceitful men.

JULIA

Crude men who use them for crude reasons! But more honest stars were in the sky when Proteus was born. He carries out what he says he will. His oaths are prophecies, his love is sincere, his thoughts are pure, his tears are honest messengers sent from his heart, and his heart is as far from lying as heaven is from earth.

LUCETTA

I pray to God he proves to be that way when you see him!

JULIA
Now, as thou lov'st me, do him not that wrong
To bear a hard opinion of his truth.
Only deserve my love by loving him,
And presently go with me to my chamber
To take a note of what I stand in need of
To furnish me upon my longing journey.
All that is mine I leave at thy dispose,
My goods, my lands, my reputation;
Only, in lieu thereof, dispatch me hence.
Come, answer not, but to it presently!
I am impatient of my tarriance.

Exeunt

ACT 2, SCENE 7
NO FEAR SHAKESPEARE

JULIA

> Now, if you love me, don't wrong him by doubting his honesty. Earn my love by loving him, and go with me right now to my bedroom to take note of what other items I need for my lovesick journey. All that I own I leave in your care, including my goods, my lands, and my reputation. Now help me leave right away. Come, don't say anything, but let's go immediately. I'm impatient from the delay.
>
> *They exit.*

ACT THREE
SCENE 1

Enter DUKE, THURIO, *and* PROTEUS

DUKE
Sir Thurio, give us leave, I pray, awhile.
We have some secrets to confer about.

Exit THURIO

Now tell me, Proteus, what's your will with me?
PROTEUS
My gracious lord, that which I would discover
The law of friendship bids me to conceal;
But when I call to mind your gracious favors
Done to me, undeserving as I am,
My duty pricks me on to utter that
Which else no worldly good should draw from me.
Know, worthy prince, Sir Valentine, my friend,
This night intends to steal away your daughter.
Myself am one made privy to the plot.
I know you have determined to bestow her
On Thurio, whom your gentle daughter hates;
And should she thus be stolen away from you,
It would be much vexation to your age.
Thus, for my duty's sake, I rather chose
To cross my friend in his intended drift
Than, by concealing it, heap on your head
A pack of sorrows which would press you down,
Being unprevented, to your timeless grave.
DUKE
Proteus, I thank thee for thine honest care,
Which to requite, command me while I live.
This love of theirs myself have often seen,
Haply when they have judged me fast asleep,

ACT THREE
SCENE 1

DUKE, THURIO, *and* PROTEUS *enter.*

DUKE

Sir Thurio, leave us alone a while, please. We have some private matters to discuss.

THURIO *exits.*

Now tell me, Proteus, why did you want to see me?

PROTEUS

My gracious lord, the rules of friendship require that I keep secret what I'm about to reveal to you. But when I think of all you've graciously done for me, undeserving as I am, my duty urges me to divulge what nothing else in the world could pull out of me. You should know, your highness, that Sir Valentine, my friend, intends to run away with your daughter tonight. I was informed of the plot. I know you've decided to marry her to Thurio, whom your lovely daughter hates. And should she be taken away from you this way, it would greatly upset you in your old age. So, for the sake of my duty, I chose to go against my friend and his intended scheme rather than hide it and burden your mind with a pack of sorrows that would weigh you down and send you to an early grave.

DUKE

Proteus, I thank you for your honest concern. In return, ask anything you want of me while I still live. I've often happened to see this love of theirs for myself, when they've thought me asleep, and frequently

      And oftentimes have purposed to forbid
      Sir Valentine her company and my court.
      But, fearing lest my jealous aim might err,
      And so, unworthily, disgrace the man—
30   A rashness that I ever yet have shunned—
      I gave him gentle looks, thereby to find
      That which thyself hast now disclosed to me.
      And, that thou mayst perceive my fear of this,
      Knowing that tender youth is soon suggested,
35   I nightly lodge her in an upper tower,
      The key whereof myself have ever kept;
      And thence she cannot be conveyed away.

PROTEUS
      Know, noble lord, they have devised a means
      How he her chamber window will ascend
40   And with a corded ladder fetch her down;
      For which the youthful lover now is gone,
      And this way comes he with it presently,
      Where, if it please you, you may intercept him.
      But, good my lord, do it so cunningly
45   That my discovery be not aimèd at;
      For, love of you, not hate unto my friend,
      Hath made me publisher of this pretence.

DUKE
      Upon mine honor, he shall never know
      That I had any light from thee of this.

PROTEUS
50   Adieu, my lord. Sir Valentine is coming.

Exit **PROTEUS**

Enter **VALENTINE** *(hurrying elsewhere, concealing a rope ladder beneath his cloak)*

DUKE
      Sir Valentine, whither away so fast?

ACT 3, SCENE 1
NO FEAR SHAKESPEARE

I've considered forbidding Sir Valentine from seeing her or attending my court. But I've been afraid my jealousy might be misplaced, and as a result I might needlessly disgrace him—I've always disdained foolish impulsiveness. So I treated him kindly, only to learn of this deceitful plot you've just revealed. And, so you know how much I fear this, I make her sleep in one of the upper towers of the castle every night, because I know how impressionable youth can be led astray. I always keep the key myself, so that she cannot be taken away.

PROTEUS
You should know, my noble lord, they have devised a way for him to climb up to her bedroom window and bring her down using a rope ladder. That's why this young lover has gone away, but he's coming back with it soon, allowing you to intercept him, if you like. But, my good lord, be cunning about it, so that he won't know I told you. It was because of my love for you, not hatred for my friend, that I told you of this plot.

DUKE
I swear on my honor he will never know I learned this information from you.

PROTEUS
Goodbye, my lord. Sir Valentine is coming.

PROTEUS exits.

VALENTINE enters (hurrying to go somewhere and concealing a rope beneath his cloak)

DUKE
Sir Valentine, what's the rush?

MODERN TEXT 105

VALENTINE
>Please it Your Grace, there is a messenger
>That stays to bear my letters to my friends,
>And I am going to deliver them.

DUKE
>Be they of much import?

VALENTINE
>The tenor of them doth but signify
>My health and happy being at your court.

DUKE
>Nay then, no matter. Stay with me awhile.
>I am to break with thee of some affairs
>That touch me near, wherein thou must be secret.
>'Tis not unknown to thee that I have sought
>To match my friend Sir Thurio to my daughter.

VALENTINE
>I know it well, my lord, and sure the match
>Were rich and honorable. Besides, the gentleman
>Is full of virtue, bounty, worth, and qualities
>Beseeming such a wife as your fair daughter.
>Cannot Your Grace win her to fancy him?

DUKE
>No, trust me. She is peevish, sullen, froward,
>Proud, disobedient, stubborn, lacking duty,
>Neither regarding that she is my child
>Nor fearing me as if I were her father.
>And, may I say to thee, this pride of hers,
>Upon advice, hath drawn my love from her;
>And, where I thought the remnant of mine age
>Should have been cherished by her childlike duty,
>I now am full resolved to take a wife,
>And turn her out to who will take her in.
>Then let her beauty be her wedding dower,
>For me and my possessions she esteems not.

VALENTINE
>What would Your Grace have me to do in this?

ACT 3, SCENE 1
NO FEAR SHAKESPEARE

VALENTINE

If you please, Your Grace, there is a messenger that waits to take my letters to my friends, and I am on my way to deliver them.

DUKE

Are they very important?

VALENTINE

In essence, they describe how healthy and happy I am here in your kingdom.

DUKE

No, then, they don't matter. Stay with me a while. I want to tell you about some affairs that affect me personally, which you must keep secret. You're surely aware that I have sought to match my friend Sir Thurio with my daughter.

VALENTINE

I know that very well, my lord, and surely the match would be profitable and honorable. Besides, the gentleman is full of virtue, wealth, worth, and qualities fit for a wife such as your beautiful daughter. Can Your Grace not get her to want him for a husband?

DUKE

No, trust me. She is irritable, sullen, difficult, proud, disobedient, stubborn, irresponsible, and neither does she care that she must obey me as my child nor does she fear me as her father. And, may I tell you, after thinking about it, this pride of hers has made me love her less. I once thought she would fulfill her duty and take care of me in my old age, but now I've resolved to find a new wife and marry my daughter off to whomever will take her. Her beauty will be her dowry, because she doesn't value me or my possessions.

VALENTINE

What part would Your Grace like me to play in this?

MODERN TEXT

DUKE
> There is a lady in Verona here
> Whom I affect, but she is nice and coy,
> And naught esteems my agèd eloquence.
> Now therefore would I have thee to my tutor—
> For long agone I have forgot to court;
> Besides, the fashion of the time is changed—
> How and which way I may bestow myself
> To be regarded in her sun-bright eye.

VALENTINE
> Win her with gifts, if she respect not words.
> Dumb jewels often in their silent kind
> More than quick words do move a woman's mind.

DUKE
> But she did scorn a present that I sent her.

VALENTINE
> A woman sometime scorns what best contents her.
> Send her another. Never give her o'er,
> For scorn at first makes after-love the more.
> If she do frown, 'tis not in hate of you,
> But rather to beget more love in you.
> If she do chide, 'tis not to have you gone,
> Forwhy the fools are mad if left alone.
> Take no repulse, whatever she doth say;
> For "Get you gone," she doth not mean "Away!"
> Flatter and praise, commend, extol their graces;
> Though ne'er so black, say they have angels' faces.
> That man that hath a tongue, I say, is no man
> If with his tongue he cannot win a woman.

DUKE
> But she I mean is promised by her friends
> Unto a youthful gentleman of worth,
> And kept severely from resort of men,
> That no man hath access by day to her.

VALENTINE
> Why then I would resort to her by night.

ACT 3, SCENE 1
NO FEAR SHAKESPEARE

DUKE

There is a lady here from Verona whom I love, but she is hard to please and coy and doesn't appreciate my old-fashioned eloquence. I'd like you to teach me how to win her over, since I long ago forgot how to court a woman, and besides, times have changed. How should I Act 1n order for her bright eyes to take notice of me?

VALENTINE

Win her with gifts if she doesn't pay attention to words. Jewels, which can't speak, often sway a woman's mind more than fast-talking.

DUKE

But she already sneered at one present I sent her.

VALENTINE

A woman will sometimes scorn the very thing that pleases her most. Send her another gift. Never give up, because her initial disdain will make her eventual feelings of love even stronger. If she frowns, it's not out of hatred for you but rather to make you love her even more. If she chides you, it's not so that you'll go away, because **the fools** will go crazy if they're left alone. Don't be offended by whatever she says. By "Get out of here," she doesn't really mean, "Go away!" Flatter and praise women, compliment them, talk about their graces. Even if they have the blackest skin, say they have the faces of angels. In my opinion, any man that has a tongue isn't really a man unless he can use it to win a woman.

That is, women.

DUKE

But the family of the woman I'm talking about has promised her to a young, worthy gentleman, and they've strictly kept her away from other men so that no man can meet with her during the day.

VALENTINE

Why, then I would see her at night.

MODERN TEXT   109

DUKE
>Ay, but the doors be locked and keys kept safe,
>That no man hath recourse to her by night.

VALENTINE
>What lets but one may enter at her window?

DUKE
>Her chamber is aloft, far from the ground,
>And built so shelving that one cannot climb it
>Without apparent hazard of his life.

VALENTINE
>Why then, a ladder quaintly made of cords
>To cast up, with a pair of anchoring hooks,
>Would serve to scale another Hero's tower,
>So bold Leander would adventure it.

DUKE
>Now, as thou art a gentleman of blood,
>Advise me where I may have such a ladder.

VALENTINE
>When would you use it? Pray, sir, tell me that.

DUKE
>This very night; for Love is like a child,
>That longs for everything that he can come by.

VALENTINE
>By seven o'clock I'll get you such a ladder.

DUKE
>But, hark thee, I will go to her alone;
>How shall I best convey the ladder thither?

VALENTINE
>It will be light, my lord, that you may bear it
>Under a cloak that is of any length.

DUKE
>A cloak as long as thine will serve the turn?

VALENTINE
>Ay, my good lord.

ACT 3, SCENE 1
NO FEAR SHAKESPEARE

DUKE

Yes, but the doors are locked and the keys tightly guarded so that no man has access to her at night.

VALENTINE

What's stopping anyone from entering her room through the window?

DUKE

Her room is high up, far from the ground, and it projects out like a shelf so that one cannot climb it without risking his life.

VALENTINE

Why then, a skillfully made ladder of rope to toss up, with a pair of grappling hooks to anchor it, would work to scale this **new Hero's tower**, allowing another daring Leander to climb it.

In Greek mythology, Hero and Leander were lovers. Leander would swim across the Hellespont each night to see her, guided by a light she set at the top of a tower.

DUKE

Now, from one nobleman by birth to another, tell me where I can get such a ladder.

VALENTINE

When would you need to use it? Please, sir, tell me that.

DUKE

Tonight, because Love is like a child that wants everything he sees.

VALENTINE

I'll get you such a ladder by seven o'clock.

DUKE

But listen, I will go see her alone. What's the best way to carry the ladder there?

VALENTINE

It will be so light, my lord, that you'll be able to carry it under any size cloak.

DUKE

A cloak as long as yours will do?

VALENTINE

Yes, my lord.

DUKE
                    Then let me see thy cloak.
I'll get me one of such another length.

VALENTINE
Why, any cloak will serve the turn, my lord.

DUKE
How shall I fashion me to wear a cloak?
I pray thee, let me feel thy cloak upon me.
                    (He pulls open VALENTINE's cloak.)
What letter is this same? What's here? "To Sylvia"!
And here an engine fit for my proceeding.
I'll be so bold to break the seal for once.

(Reads.)

My thoughts do harbor with my Sylvia nightly,
And slaves they are to me, that send them flying.
O, could their master come and go as lightly,
Himself would lodge where, senseless, they are lying!
My herald thoughts in thy pure bosom rest them,
While I, their king, that thither them importune,
Do curse the grace that with such grace hath blest them,
Because myself do want my servants' fortune.
I curse myself, for they are sent by me,
That they should harbor where their lord should be.
What's here?
Sylvia, this night I will enfranchise thee.
'Tis so; and here's the ladder for the purpose.
Why, Phaëthon, for thou art Merops' son
Wilt thou aspire to guide the heavenly car
And with thy daring folly burn the world?
Wilt thou reach stars because they shine on thee?
Go, base intruder, overweening slave!
Bestow thy fawning smiles on equal mates,
And think my patience, more than thy desert,
Is privilege for thy departure hence.
Thank me for this more than for all the favors
Which, all too much, I have bestowed on thee.

ACT 3, SCENE 1
NO FEAR SHAKESPEARE

DUKE

Then let me see your cloak. I'll get one of that same length.

VALENTINE

Why, any cloak will work just fine, my lord.

DUKE

How will I get used to wearing a cloak? Please, let me try on your cloak.

(He pulls open VALENTINE'S cloak.)

What's this letter? What does it say? "To Sylvia"! And a tool for climbing like the kind you suggested. I'll be so bold as to break the seal.

(He reads.)

"My thoughts are with my Sylvia every night. They are like my slaves, and I send them flying. Oh, I wish that I could come and go to her just as easily, and lie where my thoughts, which cannot feel, are lying. Let my thoughts, which come to you as my messengers, rest in your breast, while I, their king who sent them, curse the luck that has blessed them with such favor. I want to be as fortunate as my slaves. I curse myself, too, because I sent them to the place where I, their lord, should be." What's this here at the end? *"Sylvia, this night I will free you."* So that's it, and here's the ladder you planned to use. Why, **Phaethon—for you are Merops' son**—will you try to drive the sun god's chariot and burn the world in your brash idiocy? Will you grasp at the stars because they shine on you, as you grasp at my daughter for favoring you? Go, vulgar intruder, arrogant slave! Flash your fawning smiles on someone in your own class, and know that my patience—which is more than you deserve—allows you to leave this place. Thank me for this more than you've thanked me for all the favors I've granted you, which were too many. But if you stay here in my kingdom any longer than it takes to hurry away, then

In Greek mythology, Phaethon set the world on fire when he accidentally drove the chariot of his father, Helios, the sun god, too close to the earth. The Duke may refer to Valentine as "Merops' son" as a way of calling him an illegitimate child, because even though Phaethon's mother was married to Merops, she had Phaethon with Helios.

>   But if thou linger in my territories
> 165   Longer than swiftest expedition
>   Will give thee time to leave our royal court,
>   By heaven, my wrath shall far exceed the love
>   I ever bore my daughter or thyself.
>   Begone! I will not hear thy vain excuse,
> 170   But, as thou lov'st thy life, make speed from hence.

Exit DUKE

VALENTINE
>   And why not death rather than living torment?
>   To die is to be banished from myself,
>   And Sylvia is myself. Banished from her
>   Is self from self—a deadly banishment!
> 175   What light is light, if Sylvia be not seen?
>   What joy is joy, if Sylvia be not by?
>   Unless it be to think that she is by
>   And feed upon the shadow of perfection.
>   Except I be by Sylvia in the night,
> 180   There is no music in the nightingale;
>   Unless I look on Sylvia in the day,
>   There is no day for me to look upon.
>   She is my essence, and I leave to be
>   If I be not by her fair influence
> 185   Fostered, illumined, cherished, kept alive.
>   I fly not death, to fly his deadly doom;
>   Tarry I here, I but attend on death,
>   But, fly I hence, I fly away from life.

Enter PROTEUS *and* LAUNCE

PROTEUS
>   Run, boy, run, run, and seek him out.

LAUNCE
> 190   So-ho, so-ho!

PROTEUS
>   What seest thou?

ACT 3, SCENE 1

NO FEAR SHAKESPEARE

by heaven my anger will be far greater than any love
I've ever felt for my daughter or for you. Get out of
here! I will not hear your futile excuses. If you love
your life, then you'll hurry on your way from here.

The DUKE *exits.*

VALENTINE

Why not death instead of being tortured alive? To die
is to be banished from myself, and Sylvia is my very
being. Being banished from her is like being banished
from myself—a deadly banishment! What good is light if
I can't see Sylvia? What joy is joy if Sylvia isn't nearby?
Unless I can be happy to think she is near and live on
the mere thought of her perfection. Unless I can be near
Sylvia in the night, there is no music in the nightingale's
singing. Unless I can look on Sylvia in the day, the day
doesn't even exist. She is my essence, and I'll cease to
exist if I'm not cared for, shined upon, valued, and kept
alive by her gentle power. I don't run from death if I run
from the Duke's deadly threats. If I stay here, I am just
waiting for death, but if I flee this place, then I flee from
life itself.

PROTEUS *and* LAUNCE *enter.*

PROTEUS
Run, boy, run, run, and find him.
LAUNCE
I found him! I found him!
PROTEUS
What do you see?

LAUNCE
>Him we go to find. There's not a hair on 's head but 'tis a Valentine.

PROTEUS
>Valentine?

VALENTINE
>195 No.

PROTEUS
>Who then? His spirit?

VALENTINE
>Neither.

PROTEUS
>What then?

VALENTINE
>Nothing.

LAUNCE
>200 Can nothing speak? Master, shall I strike?

PROTEUS
>Who wouldst thou strike?

LAUNCE
>Nothing.

PROTEUS
>Villain, forbear.

LAUNCE
>Why, sir, I'll strike nothing. I pray you—

PROTEUS
>205 Sirrah, I say, forbear.—Friend Valentine, a word.

VALENTINE
>My ears are stopped and cannot hear good news,
>So much of bad already hath possessed them.

PROTEUS
>Then in dumb silence will I bury mine,
>For they are harsh, untuneable, and bad.

VALENTINE
>210 Is Sylvia dead?

ACT 3, SCENE 1
NO FEAR SHAKESPEARE

LAUNCE
> The man we were looking for. It's a Valentine, down to the last hair.

PROTEUS
> Valentine?

VALENTINE
> No.

PROTEUS
> Who are you then? His ghost?

VALENTINE
> Not his ghost either.

PROTEUS
> What are you then?

VALENTINE
> Nothing.

LAUNCE
> Can "nothing" speak? Master, should I attack?

PROTEUS
> Who would you attack?

LAUNCE
> "Nothing."

PROTEUS
> Stop, man.

LAUNCE
> But, sir, I'm going to attack "nothing." Please—

PROTEUS
> Man, I say stop. Valentine, my friend, let's talk.

VALENTINE
> My ears are plugged up and cannot hear good news— they are already filled with bad news.

PROTEUS
> Then I'll stay silent and not tell you, because my news is harsh, uncomfortable to hear, and bad.

VALENTINE
> Is Sylvia dead?

MODERN TEXT

PROTEUS
    No, Valentine.

VALENTINE
    No Valentine, indeed, for sacred Sylvia.
    Hath she forsworn me?

PROTEUS
    No, Valentine.

VALENTINE
215   No Valentine, if Sylvia have forsworn me.
    What is your news?

LAUNCE
    Sir, there is a proclamation that you are vanished.

PROTEUS
    That thou art banished—O, that's the news!—
    From hence, from Sylvia, and from me thy friend.

VALENTINE
220   O, I have fed upon this woe already,
    And now excess of it will make me surfeit.
    Doth Sylvia know that I am banished?

PROTEUS
    Ay, ay; and she hath offered to the doom—
    Which, unreversed, stands in effectual force—
225   A sea of melting pearl, which some call tears.
    Those at her father's churlish feet she tendered;
    With them, upon her knees, her humble self,
    Wringing her hands, whose whiteness so became them
    As if but now they waxed pale for woe.
230   But neither bended knees, pure hands held up,
    Sad sighs, deep groans, nor silver-shedding tears
    Could penetrate her uncompassionate sire,
    But Valentine, if he be ta'en, must die.
    Besides, her intercession chafed him so,
235   When she for thy repeal was suppliant,
    That to close prison he commanded her,
    With many bitter threats of biding there.

ACT 3, SCENE 1
NO FEAR SHAKESPEARE

PROTEUS
>No, Valentine.

VALENTINE
>There is no Valentine, indeed, for sacred Sylvia. Has she renounced her love for me?

PROTEUS
>No, Valentine.

VALENTINE
>There's no Valentine if Sylvia ever stops loving me. What's your news?

LAUNCE
>Sir, there's been an announcement that you are banished.

PROTEUS
>That you are banished. Oh, that's the news! Banished from here, from Sylvia, and from me, your friend.

VALENTINE
>Oh, I've already had my fill of this awful news, and now hearing more of it will make me sick. Does Sylvia know that I'm banished?

PROTEUS
>Yes, yes, and she's responded to the sentence—which, if not revoked, will be enforced—by crying a sea of melting pearls, which some people call tears. She cried them out at the feet of her ill-mannered father, and did so upon her knees, wringing her hands, whose beautiful whiteness appropriately seemed to result from her sorrow. But neither begging on her knees, nor extending her pure hands, nor heaving sad sighs, deep groans, or crying tears that flow like silver streams would move her unsympathetic father to change his order that Valentine must die if captured. Besides, her begging to repeal the order of banishment against you bothered him so much that he ordered her locked away and threatened to keep her there permanently.

MODERN TEXT

VALENTINE
    No more, unless the next word that thou speak'st
    Have some malignant power upon my life!
    If so, I pray thee, breathe it in mine ear,
    As ending anthem of my endless dolor.

PROTEUS
    Cease to lament for that thou canst not help,
    And study help for that which thou lament'st.
    Time is the nurse and breeder of all good.
    Here if thou stay thou canst not see thy love;
    Besides, thy staying will abridge thy life.
    Hope is a lover's staff; walk hence with that
    And manage it against despairing thoughts.
    Thy letters may be here, though thou art hence,
    Which, being writ to me, shall be delivered
    Even in the milk-white bosom of thy love.
    The time now serves not to expostulate.
    Come, I'll convey thee through the city gate,
    And, ere I part with thee confer at large
    Of all that may concern thy love affairs.
    As thou lov'st Sylvia, though not for thyself,
    Regard thy danger, and along with me!

VALENTINE
    I pray thee, Launce, an if thou seest my boy,
    Bid him make haste and meet me at the north gate.

PROTEUS
    Go, sirrah, find him out.—Come, Valentine.

VALENTINE
    O my dear Sylvia! Hapless Valentine!

                        Exeunt VALENTINE *and* PROTEUS

LAUNCE
    I am but a fool, look you, and yet I have the wit to think
    my master is a kind of a knave. But that's all one, if he be
    but one knave. He lives not now that knows me to be in
    love, yet I am in love. But a team of horse shall not pluck

ACT 3, SCENE 1
NO FEAR SHAKESPEARE

VALENTINE

Don't say any more, or the next word you say may kill me! If so, I beg you to whisper it into my ear as a final hymn for my endless misery.

PROTEUS

Stop grieving over things you can't help, and think of ways to fix the things that cause you grief. Time nurtures and breeds all good things. If you stay here, you can't see your love. Besides, staying here will shorten your life. Hope is a lover's crutch—walk forward with it and use it to prop yourself up against despair. Your letters can be here though you are far away, and if you write them to me I will deliver them to the milk-white breast of your love. Now is not the time to complain. Come, I'll escort you through the city gate, and we can talk about everything concerning your love affairs before I part with you. Consider the danger you're in, if not for yourself then for your love of Sylvia, and come along with me!

VALENTINE

Please, Launce, if you see my servant boy, tell him to hurry and meet me at the north gate.

PROTEUS

Go, boy, find him. Come, Valentine.

VALENTINE

Oh, my dear Sylvia! Unlucky Valentine!

VALENTINE and PROTEUS exit.

LAUNCE

You know, I'm just a fool, but I still have enough brains to think my master is kind of a scoundrel. But it's fine if he is a scoundrel if he's only a scoundrel regarding love. No one thinks I am in love, yet I am.

Two Gentlemen of Verona Act 3, Scene

that from me, nor who 'tis I love. And yet 'tis a woman,
but what woman, I will not tell myself. And yet 'tis a
milkmaid. Yet 'tis not a maid, for she hath had gossips.
Yet 'tis a maid, for she is her master's maid, and serves
270 for wages. She hath more qualities than a water spaniel,
which is much in a bare Christian.

(Pulling out a paper.)

Here is the catalog of her condition. *Imprimis: She can
fetch and carry.* Why, a horse can do no more. Nay, a horse
cannot fetch, but only carry; therefore is she better than
275 a jade. *Item: She can milk.* Look you, a sweet virtue in a
maid with clean hands.

Enter SPEED.

SPEED

How now, Signor Launce, what news with
your mastership?

LAUNCE

With my master's ship? Why, it is at sea.

SPEED

280 Well, your old vice still: mistake the word. What news,
then, in your paper?

LAUNCE

The black'st news that ever thou heardest.

SPEED

Why, man, how black?

LAUNCE

Why, as black as ink.

SPEED

285 Let me read them.

LAUNCE

Fie on thee, jolt-head! Thou canst not read.

SPEED

Thou liest. I can.

ACT 3, SCENE 1
NO FEAR SHAKESPEARE

But a whole team of horses couldn't tear that secret, or who it is I love, out of me. And yet it's a woman, but what kind of woman I won't even say to myself. It's a milkmaid, but she's not a virgin **since she has given birth**. Yet she is a maid, because she is her master's maid and works for wages. She has more abilities than a water spaniel, which is a lot for a simple Christian. (*Pulling out a paper*) Here is a list of all her traits. (*Reads*) *"In the first place, she can fetch and carry."* Why, a horse can't do more. No, a horse can't fetch. It can only carry. Therefore, she is better than a horse. *"Also: she can milk."* Look at that! What a sweet virtue for a maid with clean hands.

> The term "gossips" in Shakespeare's original language refers to women who assist in childbirth and the people who serve as sponsors in the baptism of a newborn, suggesting that the woman has had a child.

SPEED *enters*.

SPEED

How goes it, Signor Launce? Any news of your mastership?

LAUNCE

About my master's ship? Well, it's at sea.

SPEED

There you go again—you misunderstand me. What news is that, then, on your piece of paper?

LAUNCE

The darkest news that you've ever heard.

SPEED

Why, man, how dark?

LAUNCE

Well, as dark as ink.

SPEED

Let me read it.

LAUNCE

Get away, you blockhead! You can't read.

SPEED

You lie. I can.

LAUNCE
> I will try thee. Tell me this: who begot thee?

SPEED
> Marry, the son of my grandfather.

LAUNCE
> O, illiterate loiterer! It was the son of thy grandmother. This proves that thou canst not read.

SPEED
> Come, fool, come. Try me in thy paper.

LAUNCE
> There, (*Giving him the paper*) and Saint Nicholas be thy speed!

SPEED
> (*Reads.*) *Imprimis, She can milk.*

LAUNCE
> Ay, that she can.

SPEED
> *Item: She brews good ale.*

LAUNCE
> And thereof comes the proverb: *Blessing of your heart, you brew good ale.*

SPEED
> *Item: She can sew.*

LAUNCE
> That's as much as to say *Can she so?*

SPEED
> "*Item: She can knit.*"

LAUNCE
> What need a man care for a stock with a wench, when she can knit him a stock?

SPEED
> *Item: She can wash and scour.*

LAUNCE
> A special virtue, for then she need not be washed and scoured.

ACT 3, SCENE 1
NO FEAR SHAKESPEARE

LAUNCE

I'll test you. Tell me: who conceived you?

SPEED

The son of my grandfather, of course.

LAUNCE

Oh, illiterate loafer! It was the son of your grandmother. This proves that you cannot read.

SPEED

Come on, fool, come on. Test me with the paper.

LAUNCE

(*Giving him the paper*) There, and **Saint Nicholas** protect you!

Patron saint of scholars and schoolchildren.

SPEED

(*Reads*) "*In the first place, she can milk.*"

LAUNCE

Yes, that she can.

SPEED

"*Also: she can brew good beer.*"

LAUNCE

And that's where the proverb comes in—"*Blessing of your heart, you brew good ale.*"

SPEED

"*Also: she can sew.*"

LAUNCE

To that I say, "Can she so?"

SPEED

"*Also: she can knit.*"

LAUNCE

What does a man care if a girl's dowry doesn't include stockings, when she can knit him a stocking?

SPEED

"*Also: she can wash and scour.*"

LAUNCE

That's a special virtue, because then she doesn't need to be **washed and scoured to keep her in line**.

"Washed and scoured" was a slang phrase meaning "knocked down and beaten."

MODERN TEXT

SPEED

Item: She can spin.

LAUNCE

Then may I set the world on wheels, when she can spin for her living.

SPEED

Item: She hath many nameless virtues.

LAUNCE

That's as much as to say, bastard virtues, that indeed know not their fathers and therefore have no names.

SPEED

Here follow her vices.

LAUNCE

Close at the heels of her virtues.

SPEED

Item: She is not to be kissed fasting, in respect of her breath.

LAUNCE

Well, that fault may be mended with a breakfast. Read on.

SPEED

Item: She hath a sweet mouth.

LAUNCE

That makes amends for her sour breath.

SPEED

Item: She doth talk in her sleep.

LAUNCE

It's no matter for that, so she sleep not in her talk.

SPEED

Item: She is slow in words.

LAUNCE

O villain, that set this down among her vices! To be slow in words is a woman's only virtue. I pray thee, out with't, and place it for her chief virtue.

SPEED

Item: She is proud.

ACT 3, SCENE 1
NO FEAR SHAKESPEARE

SPEED

> "Also: she can spin yarn."

LAUNCE

Then I can take it easy, since she can spin for a living.

SPEED

> "Also: she has many virtues that can't be named."

LAUNCE

That's the same as saying they're bastard virtues that don't know their fathers and therefore have no names.

SPEED

Now comes a list of her vices.

LAUNCE

Following right behind her virtues.

SPEED

> "Also: she is not to be kissed while fasting, because of her bad breath."

LAUNCE

Well, that fault can be fixed with some breakfast. Read on.

SPEED

> "Also: she has a sweet tooth."

LAUNCE

That makes up for her sour breath.

SPEED

> "Also: she talks in her sleep."

LAUNCE

That doesn't matter, as long as she doesn't sleep while she talks.

SPEED

> "Also: she is slow with words."

LAUNCE

What a scoundrel who listed this among her vices! To speak little is a woman's only virtue! Please, cross that out and list it as her chief virtue.

SPEED

> "Also: she is proud."

LAUNCE

    Out with that too; it was Eve's legacy, and cannot be ta'en from her.

SPEED

    Item: She hath no teeth.

LAUNCE

    I care not for that neither, because I love crusts.

SPEED

    Item: She is curst.

LAUNCE

    Well, the best is, she hath no teeth to bite.

SPEED

    Item: She will often praise her liquor.

LAUNCE

    If her liquor be good, she shall. If she will not, I will, for good things should be praised.

SPEED

    Item: She is too liberal.

LAUNCE

    Of her tongue she cannot, for that's writ down she is slow of; of her purse she shall not, for that I'll keep shut. Now of another thing she may, and that cannot I help. Well, proceed.

SPEED

    Item: She hath more hair than wit, and more faults than hairs, and more wealth than faults.

LAUNCE

    Stop there; I'll have her; she was mine and not mine twice or thrice in that last article. Rehearse that once more.

SPEED

    Item: She hath more hair than wit—

LAUNCE

    More hair than wit? It may be: I'll prove it. The cover of the salt hides the salt, and therefore it is more than the salt; the hair that covers the wit is more than the wit, for

ACT 3, SCENE 1
NO FEAR SHAKESPEARE

LAUNCE
> Cross that out, too. It was Eve's legacy to all women, so it can't be taken from her.

SPEED
> *"Also: she has no teeth."*

LAUNCE
> I don't care about that either, because I love gums.

SPEED
> *"Also: she's a bitch."*

LAUNCE
> Well, at least she has no teeth with which to bite.

SPEED
> *"Also: she will taste and appraise her liquor before buying it."*

LAUNCE
> If her liquor is good, then she should. And if she won't, I will, because good things should be praised.

SPEED
> *"Also: she is too loose."*

LAUNCE
> That can't mean her tongue, since it's already written down that she's slow with words. And it isn't about her purse, because I'll keep that shut. Now she may be loose in another way, and that I can't help. Well, keep going.

SPEED
> *"Also: she has more hair than brains, and more faults than hair, and more wealth than faults."*

LAUNCE
> Stop right there. I'll take her. She was mine and then not mine two or three times in that last item. Repeat it once more.

SPEED
> *"Also: she has more hair than brains—"*

LAUNCE
> More hair than brains? Maybe that's so. I'll prove it. The top of a saltshaker hides the salt, so therefore it is more than the salt. The hair that covers the brains is more than

the greater hides the less. What's next?

SPEED

And more faults than hairs—

LAUNCE

That's monstrous. O, that that were out!

SPEED

And more wealth than faults.

LAUNCE

Why, that word makes the faults gracious. Well, I'll have her; an if it be a match, as nothing is impossible—

SPEED

What then?

LAUNCE

Why, then will I tell thee—that thy master stays for thee at the north gate.

SPEED

For me?

LAUNCE

For thee? Ay, who art thou? He hath stayed for a better man than thee.

SPEED

And must I go to him?

LAUNCE

Thou must run to him, for thou hast stayed so long that going will scarce serve the turn.

SPEED

Why didst not tell me sooner? Pox of your love letters!

Exit SPEED

LAUNCE

Now will he be swinged for reading my letter—an unmannerly slave, that will thrust himself into secrets! I'll after, to rejoice in the boy's correction.

Exit

ACT 3, SCENE 1
NO FEAR SHAKESPEARE

the brains, because the larger thing hides the smaller thing. Okay, what's next?

SPEED

"And more faults than hair—"

LAUNCE

That's awful. Oh, I wish that weren't on the list!

SPEED

"And more wealth than the faults."

LAUNCE

Why, that line makes the many faults a good thing. Well, I'll have her. If it is a good match, since nothing is impossible—

SPEED

What then?

LAUNCE

Why, then I'll tell you that your master is waiting for you at the north gate.

SPEED

For me?

LAUNCE

For you? Yeah, who are you? He's been waiting for a better man than you.

SPEED

And I have to go to him?

LAUNCE

You must run to him, because you have stayed so long that simply walking isn't going to cut it.

SPEED

Why didn't you tell me sooner? A disease take your love letters!

SPEED exits.

LAUNCE

Now he'll get beaten for reading my letter. What a rude slave for having stuck his nose in someone else's secrets. I'll follow after him, to rejoice in seeing his master whip him.

He exits.

ACT 3, SCENE 2

Enter DUKE *and* THURIO

DUKE
    Sir Thurio, fear not but that she will love you,
    Now Valentine is banished from her sight.
THURIO
    Since his exile she hath despised me most,
    Forsworn my company and railed at me,
    That I am desperate of obtaining her.
DUKE
    This weak impress of love is as a figure
    Trenchèd in ice, which with an hour's heat
    Dissolves to water and doth lose his form.
    A little time will melt her frozen thoughts,
    And worthless Valentine shall be forgot.

Enter PROTEUS.

    How now, Sir Proteus? Is your countryman,
    According to our proclamation, gone?
PROTEUS
    Gone, my good lord.
DUKE
    My daughter takes his going grievously.
PROTEUS
    A little time, my lord, will kill that grief.
DUKE
    So I believe, but Thurio thinks not so.
    Proteus, the good conceit I hold of thee—
    For thou hast shown some sign of good desert—
    Makes me the better to confer with thee.
PROTEUS
    Longer than I prove loyal to Your Grace
    Let me not live to look upon Your Grace.

ACT 3, SCENE 2

The DUKE *and* THURIO *enter.*

DUKE

Sir Thurio, don't worry. She is sure to love you now that Valentine has been banished from her sight.

THURIO

Since his exile she has despised me even more, she has refused to be around me, and she has condemned me, so that I have no hope of winning her.

DUKE

The weak impression love makes on the heart is like an ice sculpture, which melts into water and loses its form after being exposed to heat for just an hour. A little time will ease her disdain, and worthless Valentine will be forgotten.

PROTEUS *enters*

How's it going, Sir Proteus? Is your countryman gone, as our proclamation commands?

PROTEUS

He's gone, my good lord.

DUKE

My daughter is upset over his departure.

PROTEUS

A little time, my lord, will kill that grief.

DUKE

That's what I believe, too, but Thurio doesn't think so. Proteus, the high esteem I have for you—for you've shown me that you deserve it—makes me more inclined to discuss this matter with you.

PROTEUS

Let me die if I ever live to see the day I am disloyal to Your Grace.

DUKE
>Thou know'st how willingly I would effect
>The match between Sir Thurio and my daughter.

PROTEUS
>I do, my lord.

DUKE
>25 And also, I think, thou art not ignorant
>How she opposes her against my will.

PROTEUS
>She did, my lord, when Valentine was here.

DUKE
>Ay, and perversely she persevers so.
>What might we do to make the girl forget
>30 The love of Valentine, and love Sir Thurio?

PROTEUS
>The best way is to slander Valentine
>With falsehood, cowardice, and poor descent,
>Three things that women highly hold in hate.

DUKE
>Ay, but she'll think that it is spoke in hate.

PROTEUS
>35 Ay, if his enemy deliver it;
>Therefore it must with circumstance be spoken
>By one whom she esteemeth as his friend.

DUKE
>Then you must undertake to slander him.

PROTEUS
>And that, my lord, I shall be loath to do.
>40 'Tis an ill office for a gentleman,
>Especially against his very friend.

DUKE
>Where your good word cannot advantage him,
>Your slander never can endamage him;
>Therefore the office is indifferent,
>45 Being entreated to it by your friend.

ACT 3, SCENE 2
NO FEAR SHAKESPEARE

DUKE
> You know how much I would like to arrange a marriage between Sir Thurio and my daughter.

PROTEUS
> I do, my lord.

DUKE
> And also, I think, you're aware that she refuses to obey my will?

PROTEUS
> She refused when Valentine was here, my lord.

DUKE
> Yes, and oddly enough she continues to oppose me. What can we do to make this girl forget her love for Valentine and love Sir Thurio?

PROTEUS
> The best way is to slander Valentine and make up lies about his infidelity, cowardice, and poor parentage—three things women strongly hate.

DUKE
> Yes, but she'll think these things are only said out of hatred for him.

PROTEUS
> Yes, if his enemy tells her these things. Therefore, someone she believes to be his friend must tell her the details.

DUKE
> Then you must make it your job to slander him.

PROTEUS
> I would hate to do that, my lord. It's a job unsuitable for a gentleman, especially against his own friend.

DUKE
> If your praise can't help him, then your slander can't do him any harm. Therefore the task is neither good nor bad, since I, your friend, ask you to do it.

PROTEUS
>You have prevailed, my lord. If I can do it
>By aught that I can speak in his dispraise,
>She shall not long continue love to him.
>But say this weed her love from Valentine,
>It follows not that she will love Sir Thurio.

THURIO
>Therefore, as you unwind her love from him,
>Lest it should ravel and be good to none,
>You must provide to bottom it on me;
>Which must be done by praising me as much
>As you in worth dispraise Sir Valentine.

DUKE
>And, Proteus, we dare trust you in this kind
>Because we know, on Valentine's report,
>You are already Love's firm votary
>And cannot soon revolt and change your mind.
>Upon this warrant shall you have access
>Where you with Sylvia may confer at large;
>For she is lumpish, heavy, melancholy,
>And, for your friend's sake, will be glad of you,
>Where you may temper her by your persuasion
>To hate young Valentine and love my friend.

PROTEUS
>As much as I can do, I will effect.
>But you, Sir Thurio, are not sharp enough;
>You must lay lime to tangle her desires
>By wailful sonnets, whose composèd rhymes
>Should be full-fraught with serviceable vows.

DUKE
>Ay, much is the force of heaven-bred poesy.

PROTEUS
>Say that upon the altar of her beauty
>You sacrifice your tears, your sighs, your heart.
>Write till your ink be dry, and with your tears
>Moist it again, and frame some feeling line

ACT 3, SCENE 2
NO FEAR SHAKESPEARE

PROTEUS

You've convinced me, my lord. If I do what I can to speak against him, she won't love him much longer. But even if she stops loving Valentine, it doesn't mean she will love Sir Thurio.

THURIO

So, as you break down her love for him, you must build it back up around me, so that it doesn't come apart and become useless to everyone. You must do this by praising me as much as you dispraise Sir Valentine.

DUKE

And, Proteus, we feel we can trust you with this task because we know, from what Valentine told us, that you're already in love and can't quickly fall out of love. For this reason you will be allowed to speak to Sylvia as you like. She is sad, sullen, and melancholy, and she'll be happy to see you because you're close to Valentine. Then you can shape her by your persuasion to hate young Valentine and love my friend, Sir Thurio.

PROTEUS

I will do as much as I can. But you, Sir Thurio, aren't doing enough to win her. To entice her and capture her desires, you must write sonnets whose well-crafted rhymes should be filled with vows of devotion.

DUKE

Yes, poetry bred by heaven is very powerful.

PROTEUS

Say that you sacrifice your tears, your sighs, and your heart on the altar of her beauty. Write until your ink dries up and then moisten it again with your tears, and craft some emotional line that reveals your

That may discover such integrity:
For Orpheus' lute was strung with poets' sinews,
Whose golden touch could soften steel and stones,
Make tigers tame, and huge leviathans
Forsake unsounded deeps to dance on sands.
After your dire-lamenting elegies,
Visit by night your lady's chamber window
With some sweet consort. To their instruments
Tune a deploring dump; the night's dead silence
Will well become such sweet-complaining grievance.
This, or else nothing, will inherit her.

DUKE
This discipline shows thou hast been in love.

THURIO
And thy advice this night I'll put in practice.
Therefore, sweet Proteus, my direction-giver,
Let us into the city presently
To sort some gentlemen well skilled in music.
I have a sonnet that will serve the turn
To give the onset to thy good advice.

DUKE
About it, gentlemen!

PROTEUS
We'll wait upon Your Grace till after supper,
And afterward determine our proceedings.

DUKE
Even now about it! I will pardon you.

Exeunt

ACT 3, SCENE 2
NO FEAR SHAKESPEARE

sincerity—after all, **Orpheus's lute** was made from the same stuff as poetry and could soften steel and stones, make tigers tame, and cause huge whales to leave the deep ocean and dance on the sand. After you give her your love poems, go to her bedroom window at night with a group of musicians. While they play, sing a sad melody, and the silent night will enhance such sweet heartsick yearning. If that doesn't win her, nothing will.

> In Greek mythology, Orpheus was known as such a masterful musician that animals and even inanimate objects would follow him. He played the lute, a stringed instrument played by plucking.

DUKE

Your instructions show that you've been in love before.

THURIO

And I'll act on your advice tonight. Therefore, good Proteus, my guide, let's go into the city to find some gentlemen skilled at playing instruments. I have a sonnet that will work to set your plan into action.

DUKE

Let's do it, gentlemen!

PROTEUS

We'll visit Your Grace after supper and then determine our next move.

DUKE

Like I said, let's do it! You're excused.

They exit.

MODERN TEXT

ACT FOUR
SCENE 1

Enter certain OUTLAWS

FIRST OUTLAW
Fellows, stand fast. I see a passenger.
SECOND OUTLAW
If there be ten, shrink not, but down with 'em.

Enter VALENTINE *and* SPEED.

THIRD OUTLAW
Stand, sir! And throw us that you have about ye.
If not, we'll make you sit, and rifle you.
SPEED
5   Sir, we are undone. These are the villains
That all the travelers do fear so much.
VALENTINE
My friends—
FIRST OUTLAW
That's not so, sir. We are your enemies.
SECOND OUTLAW
Peace! We'll hear him.
THIRD OUTLAW
10   Ay, by my beard will we, for he is a proper man.
VALENTINE
Then know that I have little wealth to lose.
A man I am, crossed with adversity;
My riches are these poor habiliments,
Of which if you should here disfurnish me
15   You take the sum and substance that I have.
SECOND OUTLAW
Whither travel you?

ACT FOUR
SCENE 1

Several OUTLAWS *enter.*

FIRST OUTLAW
Men, get ready. I see a traveler.

SECOND OUTLAW
Even if there are ten of them, don't back down. Take them down.

VALENTINE *and* SPEED *enter.*

THIRD OUTLAW
Stop, sir! Give us what you have on you. If you don't, we'll make you sit and we'll search you.

SPEED
Sir, we're ruined. These are the bandits that all the travelers in this area fear so much.

VALENTINE
My friends—

FIRST OUTLAW
That's not how it is, sir. We are your enemies.

SECOND OUTLAW
Quiet! Let's hear him out.

THIRD OUTLAW
Yeah, by the hair on my chin we'll hear him out, because he is a handsome man.

VALENTINE
You should know that I have little wealth to lose. I am a man who's been struck by hardship. My only riches are these poor clothes I'm wearing, and if you take them then you take the sum total of everything I own.

SECOND OUTLAW
Where are you going?

VALENTINE
    To Verona.
FIRST OUTLAW
    Whence came you?
VALENTINE
    From Milan.
THIRD OUTLAW
    Have you long sojourned there?
VALENTINE
    Some sixteen months, and longer might have stayed
    If crooked fortune had not thwarted me.
FIRST OUTLAW
    What! were you banished thence?
VALENTINE
    I was.
SECOND OUTLAW
    For what offence?
VALENTINE
    For that which now torments me to rehearse:
    I killed a man, whose death I much repent,
    But yet I slew him manfully in fight
    Without false vantage or base treachery.
FIRST OUTLAW
    Why, ne'er repent it, if it were done so.
    But were you banished for so small a fault?
VALENTINE
    I was, and held me glad of such a doom.
SECOND OUTLAW
    Have you the tongues?
VALENTINE
    My youthful travel therein made me happy,
    Or else I often had been miserable.
THIRD OUTLAW
    By the bare scalp of Robin Hood's fat friar,
    This fellow were a king for our wild faction!

ACT 4, SCENE 1
NO FEAR SHAKESPEARE

VALENTINE
> To Verona.

FIRST OUTLAW
> Where did you come from?

VALENTINE
> From Milan.

THIRD OUTLAW
> How long were you there?

VALENTINE
> About sixteen months, and I might have stayed longer if bad luck hadn't thwarted me.

FIRST OUTLAW
> What! Were you banished?

VALENTINE
> I was.

SECOND OUTLAW
> For what crime?

VALENTINE
> For something that now hurts me to repeat: I killed a man, whose death I greatly regret, even though I killed him in a fair fight without deceit or wicked treachery.

FIRST OUTLAW
> Why, never regret it if that's the way it happened. Were you really banished for such a small offense?

VALENTINE
> I was, and was grateful to have just been banished.

SECOND OUTLAW
> Do you speak any other languages?

VALENTINE
> I traveled when I was young, which made me happy. Otherwise, I would have been miserable.

THIRD OUTLAW
> By the bald head of Robin Hood's fat Friar Tuck! This fellow would make a great king for our group of bandits!

FIRST OUTLAW
　　We'll have him. Sirs, a word.
　　　　　　　　(The OUTLAWS *confer in whispers.)*
SPEED
　　Master, be one of them.
40　　It's an honorable kind of thievery.
VALENTINE
　　Peace, villain!
SECOND OUTLAW
　　(Returning to Valentine)
　　Tell us this: have you anything to take to?
VALENTINE
　　Nothing but my fortune.
THIRD OUTLAW
45　　Know, then, that some of us are gentlemen,
　　Such as the fury of ungoverned youth
　　Thrust from the company of awful men.
　　Myself was from Verona banishèd
　　For practicing to steal away a lady,
50　　An heir, and near allied unto the Duke.
SECOND OUTLAW
　　And I from Mantua, for a gentleman
　　Who, in my mood, I stabbed unto the heart.
FIRST OUTLAW
　　And I for suchlike petty crimes as these.
　　But to the purpose—for we cite our faults
55　　That they may hold excused our lawless lives;
　　And partly, seeing you are beautified
　　With goodly shape, and by your own report
　　A linguist, and a man of such perfection
　　As we do in our quality much want—
SECOND OUTLAW
60　　Indeed, because you are a banished man,
　　Therefore, above the rest, we parley to you.
　　Are you content to be our general?
　　To make a virtue of necessity
　　And live, as we do, in this wilderness?

NO FEAR SHAKESPEARE

FIRST OUTLAW

We'll take him. Sirs, a word with you all.

(The OUTLAWS *confer in whispers.)*

SPEED

Master, become one of them. It's an honorable kind of thievery.

VALENTINE

Quiet, rascal!

SECOND OUTLAW

(Returning to Valentine) Tell us this: do you have any way to support yourself?

VALENTINE

Nothing but my luck.

THIRD OUTLAW

You should know, then, that some of us are gentlemen who were forced out of respectable society by our unrestrained youth. I myself was banished from Verona for planning to elope with a lady, an heir who was close to the Duke.

SECOND OUTLAW

And I am from Mantua. I stabbed a gentleman in the heart out of anger.

FIRST OUTLAW

And I was banished for such petty crimes like these. But to get to the point, we state our crimes in part because they explain why we live lives of lawlessness, and also partly because seeing that you're attractive, and by your own description a linguist, and since we are in need of a man of such qualities in our profession—

SECOND OUTLAW

In fact, because you are a banished man, and for that more than any other reason, we'd like to speak to you. Would you like to be our leader, to consider poverty an asset, and live as we do in this forest?

THIRD OUTLAW

What sayst thou? Wilt thou be of our consort?
Say ay, and be the captain of us all.
We'll do thee homage, and be ruled by thee,
Love thee as our commander and our king.

FIRST OUTLAW

But if thou scorn our courtesy thou diest.

SECOND OUTLAW

Thou shalt not live to brag what we have offered.

VALENTINE

I take your offer and will live with you,
Provided that you do no outrages
On silly women or poor passengers.

THIRD OUTLAW

No, we detest such vile base practices.
Come, go with us. We'll bring thee to our crews
And show thee all the treasure we have got,
Which, with ourselves, all rest at thy dispose.

Exeunt

ACT 4, SCENE 1
NO FEAR SHAKESPEARE

THIRD OUTLAW

What do you say? Will you join our band of highwaymen? Say yes, and become our captain. We'll respect you, be ruled by you, and love you as our leader and our king.

FIRST OUTLAW

But if you reject our offer you die.

SECOND OUTLAW

You won't live to brag about what we've offered.

VALENTINE

I accept your offer and will live with you, provided that you do not harm any helpless women or poor passengers.

THIRD OUTLAW

No, we detest such vile, wicked practices. Come, go with us. We'll take you to the rest of our band and show you all the treasure we have, which along with ourselves is at your disposal.

They exit.

ACT 4, SCENE 2

Enter PROTEUS

PROTEUS
Already have I been false to Valentine,
And now I must be as unjust to Thurio.
Under the color of commending him,
I have access my own love to prefer.
But Sylvia is too fair, too true, too holy
To be corrupted with my worthless gifts.
When I protest true loyalty to her,
She twits me with my falsehood to my friend.
When to her beauty I commend my vows,
She bids me think how I have been forsworn
In breaking faith with Julia, whom I loved.
And notwithstanding all her sudden quips,
The least whereof would quell a lover's hope,
Yet, spaniel-like, the more she spurns my love,
The more it grows and fawneth on her still.
But here comes Thurio. Now must we to her window
And give some evening music to her ear.

Enter THURIO *and* MUSICIANS

THURIO
How now, Sir Proteus, are you crept before us?
PROTEUS
Ay, gentle Thurio, for you know that love
Will creep in service where it cannot go.
THURIO
Ay, but I hope, sir, that you love not here.
PROTEUS
Sir, but I do, or else I would be hence.
THURIO
Who? Sylvia?

ACT 4, SCENE 2

PROTEUS *enters.*

PROTEUS
> I've already had to lie to Valentine, and now I must be just as unfair to Thurio. Under the guise of praising him, I now have the ability to express my own feelings of love to Sylvia. But Sylvia is too beautiful, too faithful, too holy to be corrupted by my worthless praises. When I declare my loyalty to her, she criticizes me for being false to my friend, Valentine. When I praise her beauty, she tells me to think about how I've been unfaithful to Julia, whom I once loved. And yet, despite all of her scolding, the least of which could kill a lover's hopes, my love grows and fawns on her like a dog the more she spurns it. But here comes Thurio. Now we must go to her window and play some evening music for her to hear.

THURIO *and* MUSICIANS *enter.*

THURIO
> How's it going, Sir Proteus? Did you creep over here before us?

PROTEUS
> Yes, kind Thurio, because you know that love has to creep where it isn't allowed to walk.

THURIO
> Yes, but I hope, sir, that you aren't in love in this situation.

PROTEUS
> But I am, or else I wouldn't be here.

THURIO
> Who are you in love with? Sylvia?

PROTEUS
                Ay, Sylvia—for your sake.
THURIO
25   I thank you for your own.—Now, gentlemen,
            Let's tune, and to it lustily awhile.

> *Enter, at a distance,* HOST, *and* JULIA
> *disguised as a page. They talk apart.*

HOST
            Now, my young guest, methinks you're allycholly. I pray
            you, why is it?
JULIA
            Marry, mine Host, because I cannot be merry.
HOST
30   Come, we'll have you merry. I'll bring you where you
            shall hear music and see the gentleman that you asked for.
JULIA
            But shall I hear him speak?
HOST
            Ay, that you shall.
JULIA
            That will be music.

> *Music plays.*

HOST
35   Hark! hark!
JULIA
            Is he among these?
HOST
            Ay, but peace! Let's hear 'em.

> *Song.*

MUSICIAN
            Who is Sylvia? What is she,
                That all our swains commend her?
40   *Holy, fair, and wise is she;*
                The heaven such grace did lend her,
                    That she might admirèd be.
            Is she kind as she is fair?

ACT 4, SCENE 2
NO FEAR SHAKESPEARE

PROTEUS

Yes, Sylvia—for your sake.

THURIO

I thank you for your own sake. Now, gentlemen, let's start playing, and be sure to give it all you've got.

The HOST and JULIA enter at a distance. JULIA is disguised as a page, and they talk apart from the others.

HOST

Now, my young guest, it seems to me you feel melancholy. Please tell me, why is it?

JULIA

In fact, my host, it's because I cannot be happy.

HOST

Come, we'll make you happy. I'll take you where you shall hear music and see the gentleman that you asked for.

JULIA

But will I hear him speak?

HOST

Yes, you will.

JULIA

That's music that I hear.

Music plays.

HOST

Listen! Listen!

JULIA

Is he among these musicians?

HOST

Yes, but be quiet! Let's listen to them.

Song.

MUSICIAN

Who is Sylvia? What is she like,
   That all our young men praise her?
She is holy and fair and wise;
   And Heaven has lent her such grace
     So that she may be admired.
Is she as kind as she is beautiful?

For beauty lives with kindness.
Love doth to her eyes repair
    To help him of his blindness,
        And, being helped, inhabits there.
Then to Sylvia let us sing,
    That Sylvia is excelling.
She excels each mortal thing
    Upon the dull earth dwelling.
        To her let us garlands bring.

HOST
How now? Are you sadder than you were before? How do you, man? The music likes you not.

JULIA
You mistake; the musician likes me not.

HOST
Why, my pretty youth?

JULIA
He plays false, father.

HOST
How? Out of tune on the strings?

JULIA
Not so, but yet so false that he grieves my very heartstrings.

HOST
You have a quick ear.

JULIA
Ay, I would I were deaf; it makes me have a slow heart.

HOST
I perceive you delight not in music.

JULIA
Not a whit, when it jars so.

HOST
Hark, what fine change is in the music!

JULIA
Ay, that change is the spite.

ACT 4, SCENE 2
NO FEAR SHAKESPEARE

Because beauty and kindness are joined.
Cupid makes visits to her eyes
   To cure him of his blindness,
      And, being cured, he stays there to live.
Then let us sing to Sylvia,
   That Sylvia is superior.
She surpasses every mortal thing
   That lives on this dull earth.
      Let us bring her flower garlands.

HOST

What's this? Are you sadder than you were before? What's going on, man? You don't like the music?

JULIA

You're mistaken. The musician doesn't like me.

HOST

Why, my young friend?

JULIA

He is being false, sir.

HOST

How so? Are his instrument's strings out of tune?

JULIA

No, but he's being so false that it hurts my very heartstrings.

HOST

You have a good ear.

JULIA

Yes, but I wish I were deaf. It makes my heart sad.

HOST

I see you don't enjoy listening to music.

JULIA

Not at all, when it sounds so awful.

HOST

Listen, how they change their tune!

JULIA

Yes, that "change" is the problem.

HOST
>You would have them always play but one thing?

JULIA
>I would always have one play but one thing. But, Host, doth this Sir Proteus that we talk on often resort unto this gentlewoman?

HOST
>I tell you what Launce, his man, told me: he loved her out of all nick.

JULIA
>Where is Launce?

HOST
>Gone to seek his dog, which tomorrow, by his master's command, he must carry for a present to his lady.

JULIA
>Peace! Stand aside. The company parts.
>
>*(JULIA and the HOST stand aside.)*

PROTEUS
>Sir Thurio, fear not you. I will so plead
>That you shall say my cunning drift excels.

THURIO
>Where meet we?

PROTEUS
>At Saint Gregory's well.

THURIO
>Farewell.
>*Exeunt* THURIO *and* MUSICIANS

Enter SYLVIA *above, at her window.*

PROTEUS
>Madam, good even to your ladyship.

SYLVIA
>I thank you for your music, gentlemen.
>Who is that that spake?

ACT 4, SCENE 2
NO FEAR SHAKESPEARE

HOST
> Would you prefer that they always play just one thing?

JULIA
> I would always have one of them play only one song. But, host, does this Sir Proteus we're talking about often go to this lady?

HOST
> I'll tell you what Launce, his servant, told me: he loved her more than anything.

JULIA
> Where is Launce?

HOST
> Gone to find his dog, which he must deliver as a present to Sylvia tomorrow upon his master's command.

JULIA
> Quiet! Step aside. The musicians are leaving.
>> *(JULIA and the HOST stand aside.)*

PROTEUS
> Sir Thurio, don't worry. I will plead to Sylvia so effectively that you'll say my cunning scheme is excellent.

THURIO
> Where will we meet?

PROTEUS
> At Saint Gregory's well.

THURIO
> Farewell.
>> *THURIO and the MUSICIANS exit.*

SYLVIA enters above, at her window.

PROTEUS
> Madame, good evening to your ladyship.

SYLVIA
> I thank you for your music, sir. Who is that who spoke?

PROTEUS
85   One, lady, if you knew his pure heart's truth,
      You would quickly learn to know him by his voice.
SYLVIA
      Sir Proteus, as I take it.
PROTEUS
      Sir Proteus, gentle lady, and your servant.
SYLVIA
      What's your will?
PROTEUS
90   That I may compass yours.
SYLVIA
      You have your wish. My will is even this:
      That presently you hie you home to bed.
      Thou subtle, perjured, false, disloyal man!
      Think'st thou I am so shallow, so conceitless,
95   To be seducèd by thy flattery,
      That hast deceived so many with thy vows?
      Return, return, and make thy love amends.
      For me, by this pale queen of night I swear,
      I am so far from granting thy request
100   That I despise thee for thy wrongful suit,
      And by and by intend to chide myself
      Even for this time I spend in talking to thee.
PROTEUS
      I grant, sweet love, that I did love a lady,
      But she is dead.
JULIA
105   (*Aside*)   'Twere false, if I should speak it,
      For I am sure she is not burièd.
SYLVIA
      Say that she be, yet Valentine, thy friend,
      Survives, to whom—thyself art witness—
      I am betrothed. And art thou not ashamed
110   To wrong him with thy importunacy?

ACT 4, SCENE 2
NO FEAR SHAKESPEARE

PROTEUS

Someone, lady, whom you would quickly learn to recognize by his voice if you knew how he truly felt.

SYLVIA

Sir Proteus, I take it.

PROTEUS

Sir Proteus, gentle lady, and also your servant.

SYLVIA

What do you want?

PROTEUS

For you to want me.

SYLVIA

Then you have your wish. I want this of you: that you take yourself home to bed. You sly, lying, false, disloyal man! Do you think I'm so shallow, so stupid, that you can seduce me with your flattery when you've deceived so many others with your vows? Go back, go back, and apologize to your love. I swear on the moon, I am so far from granting your request that I despise you for your misguided plea. In a moment I intend to scold myself for spending even this much time talking to you.

PROTEUS

I admit, sweet love, that I did love a lady. But she is dead.

JULIA

(*Aside*) That's false, if I do say so myself, because I'm sure she's not dead and buried.

SYLVIA

Even if she is dead, Valentine—your friend—is still alive, and you know that I'm betrothed to him. Aren't you ashamed to wrong him with your disrespect?

MODERN TEXT

PROTEUS
　　　I likewise hear that Valentine is dead.
SYLVIA
　　　And so suppose am I, for in his grave,
　　　Assure thyself, my love is burièd.
PROTEUS
　　　Sweet lady, let me rake it from the earth.
SYLVIA
115　　Go to thy lady's grave and call hers thence.
　　　Or, at the least, in hers sepulchre thine.
JULIA
　　　(*Aside*) He heard not that.
PROTEUS
　　　Madam, if your heart be so obdurate,
　　　Vouchsafe me yet your picture for my love,
120　　The picture that is hanging in your chamber.
　　　To that I'll speak, to that I'll sigh and weep;
　　　For, since the substance of your perfect self
　　　Is else devoted, I am but a shadow,
　　　And to your shadow will I make true love.
JULIA
125　　(*Aside*) If 'twere a substance, you would, sure, deceive it,
　　　And make it but a shadow, as I am.

SYLVIA
　　　I am very loath to be your idol, sir.
　　　But since your falsehood shall become you well
　　　To worship shadows and adore false shapes,
130　　Send to me in the morning, and I'll send it.
　　　And so, good rest.
PROTEUS
　　　　　　　　　　　As wretches have o'ernight
　　　That wait for execution in the morn.
　　　　　　　　Exeunt **PROTEUS** *and* **SYLVIA** *separately*

ACT 4, SCENE 2
NO FEAR SHAKESPEARE

PROTEUS

I also hear that Valentine is dead.

SYLVIA

Then consider me dead, too, because you can be sure my love is buried with him in his grave.

PROTEUS

Sweet lady, let me dig up your love from the earth.

SYLVIA

Go to your lady's grave and dig up her love then. Or at least bury yours in her tomb.

JULIA

(*Aside*) He didn't hear that.

PROTEUS

Madame, if your heart is so stubborn, at least indulge my love by giving me a portrait of yourself—the picture that is hanging in your bedroom. I'll speak, sigh, and weep to that. Since you are completely devoted to someone else, I am nothing, and therefore I will love your image and not you.

JULIA

(*Aside*) If it were a real woman you would certainly deceive her and make her into nothing, just as I am nothing now.

SYLVIA

I don't want to be your idol, sir. But since it's appropriate that your deceiving self should worship shadows and adore images rather than the real thing, send your servant to me in the morning, and I'll send you the portrait. So go on, and good night.

PROTEUS

I'll have as good a night as the condemned man who awaits execution in the morning.

PROTEUS and SYLVIA exit separately.

JULIA
  Host, will you go?
HOST
135 By my halidom, I was fast asleep.
JULIA
  Pray you, where lies Sir Proteus?
HOST
  Marry, at my house. Trust me, I think 'tis almost day.
JULIA
  Not so; but it hath been the longest night
  That e'er I watched, and the most heaviest.

Exeunt

ACT 4, SCENE 2
NO FEAR SHAKESPEARE

JULIA

Host, are you leaving?

HOST

My goodness, I was fast asleep.

JULIA

Please, where is Sir Proteus staying?

HOST

Why, at my house. Oh my word, I think it's almost dawn.

JULIA

No, it isn't. It's been the longest night I've ever had, and the saddest.

They exit.

ACT 4, SCENE 3

Enter SIR EGLAMOUR

EGLAMOUR
>This is the hour that Madam Sylvia
>Entreated me to call and know her mind.
>There's some great matter she'd employ me in.
>Madam, madam!

Enter SYLVIA *above, at her window.*

SYLVIA
>⁵ Who calls?

EGLAMOUR
>Your servant and your friend;
>One that attends your ladyship's command.

SYLVIA
>Sir Eglamour, a thousand times good morrow.

EGLAMOUR
>As many, worthy lady, to yourself.
>¹⁰ According to your ladyship's impose,
>I am thus early come to know what service
>It is your pleasure to command me in.

SYLVIA
>O Eglamour, thou art a gentleman—
>Think not I flatter, for I swear I do not—
>¹⁵ Valiant, wise, remorseful, well accomplished.
>Thou art not ignorant what dear good will
>I bear unto the banished Valentine,
>Nor how my father would enforce me marry
>Vain Thurio, whom my very soul abhors.
>²⁰ Thyself hast loved, and I have heard thee say
>No grief did ever come so near thy heart
>As when thy lady and thy true love died,
>Upon whose grave thou vowedst pure chastity.

ACT 4, SCENE 3

SIR EGLAMOUR *enters.*

EGLAMOUR

This is the time that Madame Sylvia asked me to come by so that she could tell me something. There's an important matter she'd like my help with. Madame! Madame!

SYLVIA *enters above at her window.*

SYLVIA

Who's there?

EGLAMOUR

Your servant and your friend—one that is here to obey your ladyship's orders.

SYLVIA

Sir Eglamour, good morning a thousand times over.

EGLAMOUR

As many to you, my worthy lady. I've come as your ladyship asked and have arrived a little early to find out what you'd like me to do for you.

SYLVIA

Oh, Eglamour, you are a gentleman, valiant, wise, and very successful. Don't think I'm trying to flatter you, because I swear I'm not. I'm sure you know how dearly I feel about the banished Valentine, and how my father wants to force me to marry that conceited Thurio, whom I hate down to my very soul. You've been in love before, and I've heard you say you've never experienced more grief than when your lady and true love died. You swore a vow of chastity on her grave. Sir Eglamour, I want to go to Valentine in Mantua, where I hear he is living. Because the journey there is a dangerous one, I'd like you to

Sir Eglamour, I would to Valentine,
To Mantua, where I hear he makes abode;
And, for the ways are dangerous to pass,
I do desire thy worthy company,
Upon whose faith and honor I repose.
Urge not my father's anger, Eglamour,
But think upon my grief, a lady's grief,
And on the justice of my flying hence
To keep me from a most unholy match,
Which heaven and fortune still rewards with plagues.
I do desire thee, even from a heart
As full of sorrows as the sea of sands,
To bear me company and go with me;
If not, to hide what I have said to thee,
That I may venture to depart alone.

EGLAMOUR
Madam, I pity much your grievances,
Which, since I know they virtuously are placed,
I give consent to go along with you,
Recking as little what betideth me
As much I wish all good befortune you.
When will you go?

SYLVIA
       This evening coming.

EGLAMOUR
Where shall I meet you?

SYLVIA
       At Friar Patrick's cell,
Where I intend holy confession.

EGLAMOUR
I will not fail your ladyship.
Good morrow, gentle lady.

SYLVIA
Good morrow, kind Sir Eglamour.

Exeunt separately

accompany me, as I trust in your faith and honor. Don't use my father's anger as an excuse, Eglamour, but think about my grief—a lady's grief—and about why it's fair that I run away to avoid this terrible marriage, the kind heaven always afflicts with problems. Even though my heart is as full of sorrow as the sea is full of sand, I want you to keep me company and go with me. If you don't want to go, then please don't reveal what I've said to you, so that I can leave without anyone knowing.

EGLAMOUR

Madame, I pity you for your grievances. Since I know they are legitimate, I agree to go along with you. I'm not concerned what may happen to me, and I wish you the best of luck. When will you go?

SYLVIA

This evening.

EGLAMOUR

Where should I meet you?

SYLVIA

At Friar Patrick's chambers, where I intend to take holy confession.

EGLAMOUR

I won't fail you, your ladyship. Good day, gentle lady.

SYLVIA

Good day, kind Sir Eglamour.

They exit separately.

ACT 4, SCENE 4

Enter LAUNCE *with his dog, Crab*

LAUNCE
When a man's servant shall play the cur with him, look you, it goes hard—one that I brought up of a puppy, one that I saved from drowning when three or four of his blind brothers and sisters went to it. I have taught him, even as one would say precisely, "Thus I would teach a dog." I was sent to deliver him as a present to Mistress Sylvia from my master, and I came no sooner into the dining chamber, but he steps me to her trencher and steals her capon's leg. O, 'tis a foul thing when a cur cannot keep himself in all companies! I would have, as one should say, one that takes upon him to be a dog indeed, to be, as it were, a dog at all things. If I had not had more wit than he, to take a fault upon me that he did, I think verily he had been hanged for't; sure as I live, he had suffered for 't. You shall judge. He thrusts me himself into the company of three or four gentlemanlike dogs, under the Duke's table. He had not been there—bless the mark!—a pissing while but all the chamber smelt him. "Out with the dog!" says one; "What cur is that?" says another. "Whip him out," says the third. "Hang him up," says the Duke. I, having been acquainted with the smell before, knew it was Crab, and goes me to the fellow that whips the dogs. "Friend," quoth I, "you mean to whip the dog?" "Ay, marry do I," quoth he. "You do him the more wrong," quoth I; "'twas I did the thing you wot of." He makes me no more ado, but whips me out of the chamber. How many masters would do this for his servant? Nay, I'll be sworn I have sat in the stocks for puddings he hath stolen, otherwise he had been executed. I have stood on the pillory for geese he hath killed, otherwise he had suffered for 't.—Thou think'st not of

ACT 4, SCENE 4

LAUNCE *enters with his dog, Crab.*

LAUNCE
When a man's pet behaves like a stupid mongrel, mind you, it's hard to take—a dog that I brought up from a puppy, one that I saved from drowning when three or four of his newborn brothers and sisters were drowned. I have trained him quite literally "as I would teach a dog," as the saying goes. I was sent to deliver him as a present to Mistress Sylvia from my master, but no sooner had I stepped into the dining room than he ran ahead of me to the plate and stole her drumstick. Oh, it is a foul thing when a mongrel can't behave himself in front of company! It seems I have a dog that tries to be a dog indeed—dog-gone good at all things, as one would say. If I hadn't had the brains to take the blame for what he'd done, I honestly think he would have been hanged for it. As sure as I'm alive he would have been punished for it. You be the judge. He thrusts himself under the Duke's table and into the company of three or four fancier dogs. He hadn't been there a second or two before everyone in the whole room could smell his piss—pardon my French! "Out with the dog!" says one person; "What mangy mutt is that?" asks another. "Whip him," says a third. "Hang him!" says the Duke. I, having smelled that smell before, knew it was Crab, so I went to the fellow whose job it is to whip the dogs. "Friend," I said, "are you going to whip the dog?" "Yes, in fact, I am," he replied. "Then you're doing him a great injustice," I answered back, "because it was I who peed all over the place." He didn't say anything else but just whipped me out of the room. How many masters would do this for their pets? No, I swear I've sat in the stocks for meat pies he has stolen—otherwise he would have been executed. I have stood on

Two Gentlemen of Verona   Act 4, Scene

this now. Nay, I remember the trick you served me when
I took my leave of Madam Sylvia. Did not I bid thee
still mark me and do as I do? When didst thou see me
heave up my leg and make water against a gentlewoman's
farthingale? Didst thou ever see me do such a trick?

Enter PROTEUS *and* JULIA *(disguised)*

PROTEUS
(*To Julia*) Sebastian is thy name? I like thee well,
And will employ thee in some service presently.

JULIA
In what you please. I'll do what I can.

PROTEUS
I hope thou wilt. (*To Launce*) How now, you whoreson peasant,
Where have you been these two days loitering?

LAUNCE
Marry, sir, I carried Mistress Sylvia the dog you bade me.

PROTEUS
And what says she to my little jewel?

LAUNCE
Marry, she says your dog was a cur, and tells you currish
thanks is good enough for such a present.

PROTEUS
But she received my dog?

LAUNCE
No, indeed, did she not. Here have I brought him
back again.

(He points to his dog.)

PROTEUS
What, didst thou offer her this from me?

ACT 4, SCENE 4
NO FEAR SHAKESPEARE

the pillory for geese he has killed—otherwise he would have suffered the consequences. You don't remember any of this now, do you, Crab? No, I remember the trick you pulled on me when I said good-bye to Madame Sylvia. Didn't I tell you that you should still obey me and do as I do? When did you ever see me lift up my leg and urinate on a noble woman's undergarments? Did you ever see me do such a thing?

PROTEUS *and* JULIA *enter, she in disguise.*

PROTEUS

(*To Julia*) Your name is Sebastian, right? I like you, and I'd like to hire you for a job I need done.

JULIA

Name it. I'll do what I can.

PROTEUS

I hope you will. (*To Launce*) How's it going, you poor son of a bitch? Where have you been hanging around these past two days?

LAUNCE

Well, sir, I brought the dog to Mistress Sylvia, as you instructed.

PROTEUS

What did she say about my little jewel of a gift?

LAUNCE

Actually, she said your dog was a mongrel and said that a shabby thanks is good enough for such a present.

PROTEUS

But she accepted my dog?

LAUNCE

No, indeed, she didn't. Here, I've brought him back again.

(He points to his dog.)

PROTEUS

What, did you offer her this mutt from me?

LAUNCE
Ay, sir: the other squirrel was stolen from me by the
hangman boys in the marketplace, and then I offered
her mine own, who is a dog as big as ten of yours, and
therefore the gift the greater.

PROTEUS
55 Go get thee hence, and find my dog again,
Or ne'er return again into my sight.
Away, I say! Stayest thou to vex me here?

Exit **LAUNCE** *(with Crab)*

A slave, that still an end turns me to shame!—
Sebastian, I have entertainèd thee,
60 Partly that I have need of such a youth
That can with some discretion do my business,
For 'tis no trusting to yond foolish lout,
But chiefly for thy face and thy behavior,
Which, if my augury deceive me not,
65 Witness good bringing up, fortune, and truth.
Therefore know thou, for this I entertain thee.
Go presently, and take this ring with thee.

(Giving a ring)

Deliver it to Madam Sylvia—
She loved me well delivered it to me.

JULIA
70 It seems you loved not her, to leave her token.
She's dead, belike?

PROTEUS
                        Not so. I think she lives.

JULIA
Alas!

PROTEUS
Why dost thou cry "Alas"?

JULIA
75 I cannot choose but pity her.

PROTEUS
Wherefore shouldst thou pity her?

NO FEAR SHAKESPEARE

LAUNCE
> Yes, sir. The other runt was stolen from me by a gang of boys in the marketplace. So, I offered her my own, which is a bigger dog than ten of your little dogs, and so a better gift.

PROTEUS
> Go on and get out of here, and find my dog again, or never let me see you again. Away, I say! Are you staying here to make me angry?
>
> *LAUNCE exits with Crab.*
>
> What a scoundrel, who never fails to disgrace me! Sebastian, I've hired you partly because I have need of a young man who can take care of some business for me quietly, and there's no trusting that foolish lout Launce. But I've chiefly hired you for the way you look and act, which, if my intuition doesn't deceive me, mean you are honest, lucky, and have been brought up well. Know that this is why I hired you. Now go, and take this ring with you.
>
> *(He gives JULIA, disguised as Launce, a ring.)*
>
> The woman who gave it to me loved me very much. Deliver it to Madame Sylvia.

JULIA
> It seems you didn't love her if you're giving away her gift. Is she dead?

PROTEUS
> No. I think she's alive.

JULIA
> Oh no!

PROTEUS
> Why do you cry "Oh no!"?

JULIA
> I can't help but feel sorry for her.

PROTEUS
> Why would you feel sorry for her?

JULIA
>Because methinks that she loved you as well
>As you do love your lady Sylvia.
>She dreams on him that has forgot her love;
>You dote on her that cares not for your love.
>'Tis pity love should be so contrary;
>And thinking on it makes me cry "alas!"

PROTEUS
>Well, give her that ring and therewithal
>This letter. (*Giving a letter*) That's her chamber.
>   Tell my lady
>I claim the promise for her heavenly picture.
>Your message done, hie home unto my chamber,
>Where thou shalt find me, sad and solitary.

Exit **PROTEUS**

JULIA
>How many women would do such a message?
>Alas, poor Proteus! thou hast entertained
>A fox to be the shepherd of thy lambs.
>Alas, poor fool, why do I pity him
>That with his very heart despiseth me?
>Because he loves her, he despiseth me;
>Because I love him, I must pity him.
>This ring I gave him when he parted from me,
>To bind him to remember my good will;
>And now am I, unhappy messenger,
>To plead for that which I would not obtain,
>To carry that which I would have refused,
>To praise his faith, which I would have dispraised.
>I am my master's true-confirmèd love,
>But cannot be true servant to my master
>Unless I prove false traitor to myself.
>Yet will I woo for him, but yet so coldly
>As, heaven it knows, I would not have him speed.

ACT 4, SCENE 4
NO FEAR SHAKESPEARE

JULIA

> Because I suspect she loved you as much as you love your lady Sylvia. She dreams of that man who has forgotten her love. You dote on a woman who doesn't care for your love. It's a pity love is so difficult, and thinking about it makes me cry "Oh no!"

PROTEUS

> Well, give her that ring and with it this letter. (*Giving a letter*) That's her room. Tell her I want the heavenly picture she promised me. When you've finished delivering the message, return home to my room, where you'll find me sad and alone.

> > > > > > > > > > *PROTEUS exits.*

JULIA

> How many women would deliver such a message? Too bad, poor Proteus! You've hired a fox to be the shepherd of your lambs. Why, poor fool that I am, do I pity the man who despises me? He despises me because he loves her, and I feel sorry for him because I love him. This is the ring I gave him when he left, and it was to remind him always of my feelings. And now I'm an unhappy messenger who is supposed to ask for the picture I don't want him to have, to deliver the ring I want Sylvia to refuse, and to praise his loyalty, which I want to disparage. I am my master's true love, but I can't be a loyal servant to my master without being a traitor to myself. Still I'll woo Sylvia for him, but heaven knows I'll do it coldly, because I don't want him to win her.

Enter SYLVIA *attended*

Gentlewoman, good day! I pray you be my means
To bring me where to speak with Madam Sylvia.

SYLVIA

What would you with her, if that I be she?

JULIA

If you be she, I do entreat your patience
To hear me speak the message I am sent on.

SYLVIA

From whom?

JULIA

From my master, Sir Proteus, madam.

SYLVIA

O, he sends you for a picture?

JULIA

Ay, madam.

SYLVIA

Ursula, bring my picture there.
(A servant brings SYLVIA *a picture, which she gives to* JULIA.*)*
Go, give your master this. Tell him from me,
One Julia, that his changing thoughts forget,
Would better fit his chamber than this shadow.

JULIA

Madam, please you peruse this letter.—
(She offers a letter and withdraws it.)
Pardon me, madam; I have unadvised
Delivered you a paper that I should not.
(She gives another letter.)
This is the letter to your ladyship.

SYLVIA

I pray thee, let me look on that again.

JULIA

It may not be. Good madam, pardon me.

ACT 4, SCENE 4
NO FEAR SHAKESPEARE

SYLVIA *enters with servants.*

Gentlewoman, good day! Would you please take me to Madame Sylvia so that I may speak with her?

SYLVIA
What do you want with her, assuming I am she?

JULIA
If you are she, I ask your patience to hear me deliver the message I've been instructed to bring you.

SYLVIA
From whom?

JULIA
From my master, Sir Proteus, madame.

SYLVIA
Oh, did he send you for a picture of me?

JULIA
Yes, madame.

SYLVIA
Ursula, bring my picture there.
(*A servant brings* SYLVIA *a picture, which she gives to* JULIA.)
Go, give your master this. Tell him from me that a woman named Julia, whom his fickle heart has forgotten, would be more appropriate for his bedroom than this image of me.

JULIA
Madame, please read this letter.
(*She offers a letter, but then takes it back.*)
Pardon me, madame—I accidentally gave you a paper I shouldn't have.
(*She gives another letter.*)
This is the letter for your ladyship.

SYLVIA
Please, let me look at that other letter again.

JULIA
I can't do that. Forgive me, good madame.

SYLVIA
>There, hold!
>I will not look upon your master's lines.
>130 I know they are stuffed with protestations
>And full of newfound oaths, which he will break
>As easily as I do tear his paper.

(She tears the letter.)

JULIA
>*(Offering the ring)*
>Madam, he sends your ladyship this ring.

SYLVIA
>135 The more shame for him that he sends it me,
>For I have heard him say a thousand times
>His Julia gave it him at his departure.
>Though his false finger have profaned the ring,
>Mine shall not do his Julia so much wrong.

JULIA
>140 She thanks you.

SYLVIA
>What sayst thou?

JULIA
>I thank you, madam, that you tender her.
>Poor gentlewoman! My master wrongs her much.

SYLVIA
>Dost thou know her?

JULIA
>145 Almost as well as I do know myself.
>To think upon her woes I do protest
>That I have wept a hundred several times.

SYLVIA
>Belike she thinks that Proteus hath forsook her.

JULIA
>I think she doth, and that's her cause of sorrow.

SYLVIA
>150 Is she not passing fair?

ACT 4, SCENE 4
NO FEAR SHAKESPEARE

SYLVIA

Wait, stop! I will not look at your master's letter. I know it is filled with vows and full of newly made oaths, which he will break as easily as I tear up his letter.

(She tears the letter.)

JULIA

(*Offering the ring*) Madame, he sends your ladyship this ring.

SYLVIA

He should be even more ashamed for sending it to me, since I have heard him say a thousand times that his love Julia gave it to him when he departed. Even though his deceitful finger has sullied the ring, my finger will not mistreat Julia so much.

JULIA

She thanks you.

SYLVIA

What did you say?

JULIA

I thank you, madame, that you consider her feelings. Poor gentlewoman! My master mistreats her very much.

SYLVIA

Do you know her?

JULIA

Almost as well as I know myself. I swear I've wept several hundred times thinking about her sorrows.

SYLVIA

She probably thinks that Proteus has rejected her.

JULIA

I think she does, and that's the cause of her sorrow.

SYLVIA

Isn't she very beautiful?

JULIA
    She hath been fairer, madam, than she is.
    When she did think my master loved her well,
    She, in my judgment, was as fair as you;
    But since she did neglect her looking-glass
155   And threw her sun-expelling mask away,
    The air hath starved the roses in her cheeks
    And pinched the lily tincture of her face,
    That now she is become as black as I.

SYLVIA
    How tall was she?

JULIA
160   About my stature; for at Pentecost,
    When all our pageants of delight were played,
    Our youth got me to play the woman's part,
    And I was trimmed in Madam Julia's gown,
    Which servèd me as fit, by all men's judgments,
165   As if the garment had been made for me:
    Therefore I know she is about my height.
    And at that time I made her weep agood,
    For I did play a lamentable part:
    Madam, 'twas Ariadne passioning
170   For Theseus' perjury and unjust flight;
    Which I so lively acted with my tears
    That my poor mistress, movèd therewithal,
    Wept bitterly; and would I might be dead
    If I in thought felt not her very sorrow!

SYLVIA
175   She is beholding to thee, gentle youth.
    Alas, poor lady, desolate and left!
    I weep myself, to think upon thy words.
    Here, youth, there is my purse.
    (*She gives money.*) I give thee this
180   For thy sweet mistress' sake, because thou lov'st her.
    Farewell.

Exit **SYLVIA**, *with attendants*

ACT 4, SCENE 4
NO FEAR SHAKESPEARE

JULIA

> She has been more beautiful, madame, than she is now. When she thought my master loved her deeply, she was as beautiful as you, in my opinion. But since she no longer takes care of her appearance and has thrown her **sunblocking mask** away, the air has taken the rosiness from her cheeks and stolen the whiteness from her face, so that now she is as ugly as I am.

A mask worn by women to keep the sun off their faces.

SYLVIA

> How tall was she?

JULIA

> About my height. When we put on a pageant at **Pentecost**, the young men got me to play the part of a woman, and I was dressed in Madame Julia's gown, which everyone said fit me very well, as if the garment had been made for me. Therefore, I know she is about my height. And at the time I made her cry a lot, because I played a really sad part—I was **Ariadne**, Madame, suffering from Theseus' lies and unfair departure. I acted the part so convincingly with my tears that poor Julia, moved with the performance, wept bitterly. I would wish I were dead if I didn't feel her very sorrow!

A religious holiday period that follows seven weeks after Easter.

In Greek mythology, Ariadne fell in love with Theseus and promised to help him find his way out of the Minotaur's labyrinth if he would take her to Athens and marry her. But on the way, Theseus abandoned her, either accidentally or deliberately, depending on the account.

SYLVIA

> She is indebted to you, young man. Such a shame—the poor lady, desolate and abandoned! I weep myself just hearing your story. Here, young man, there is my purse. (*She gives him some money.*) I give this to you for your sweet mistress's sake, because you love her. Farewell.

> > > **SYLVIA** *exits with servants.*

MODERN TEXT

JULIA
And she shall thank you for't, if e'er you know her.—
A virtuous gentlewoman, mild and beautiful!
I hope my master's suit will be but cold,
Since she respects my mistress' love so much.
Alas, how love can trifle with itself!
Here is her picture. (*She looks at the picture.*)
Let me see, I think
If I had such a tire, this face of mine
Were full as lovely as is this of hers;
And yet the painter flattered her a little,
Unless I flatter with myself too much.
Her hair is auburn, mine is perfect yellow;
If that be all the difference in his love,
I'll get me such a colored periwig.
Her eyes are grey as glass, and so are mine.
Ay, but her forehead's low, and mine's as high.
What should it be that he respects in her
But I can make respective in myself,
If this fond Love were not a blinded god?
Come, shadow, come, and take this shadow up,
For 'tis thy rival. (*She picks up the picture.*)
O thou senseless form,
Thou shalt be worshiped, kissed, loved, and adored!
And, were there sense in his idolatry,
My substance should be statue in thy stead.
I'll use thee kindly for thy mistress' sake,
That used me so; or else, by Jove I vow,
I should have scratched out your unseeing eyes
To make my master out of love with thee!

Exit

ACT 4, SCENE 4
NO FEAR SHAKESPEARE

JULIA

> And she will thank you for it, if you ever meet her. A virtuous gentlewoman, kind and beautiful! I hope my master's endeavors to win her love will fail since she respects the love I feel for him so much. It's too bad how love can fool itself! Here is her picture. (*She looks at the picture.*) Let me see. I think if I had a similar headdress my face would be as lovely as hers. And yet the painter made her prettier than she is, unless I flatter myself too much in thinking I'm as pretty. Her hair is auburn, while mine is perfect yellow. If that's the only thing he likes better about her, then I'll get myself a blond wig. Her eyes are as gray as glass, and so are mine. Yes, but her forehead's low, and mine is as high as hers is low. If Love is really blind, what does he value in her that I can't make him value in myself? Let's go, Sebastian. Let's go and get rid of this picture, since it's your rival. (*She picks up the picture.*) Oh you unfeeling image, you'll be worshiped, kissed, loved, and adored! Were there any sense in his worship, it would be the real me he worships instead. I'll treat this picture kindly for the sake of its mistress, who treated me so well. Otherwise, by Jove, I would have scratched out your unseeing eyes to make my master fall out of love with you!
>
> *Exit.*

MODERN TEXT

ACT FIVE
SCENE 1

Enter SIR EGLAMOUR

EGLAMOUR
>The sun begins to gild the western sky,
>And now it is about the very hour
>That Sylvia at Friar Patrick's cell should meet me.
>She will not fail, for lovers break not hours
>Unless it be to come before their time,
>So much they spur their expedition.

Enter SYLVIA

>See, where she comes.—Lady, a happy evening!

SYLVIA
>Amen, amen! Go on, good Eglamour,
>Out at the postern by the abbey wall.
>I fear I am attended by some spies.

EGLAMOUR
>Fear not. The forest is not three leagues off.
>If we recover that, we are sure enough.

Exeunt

ACT FIVE
SCENE 1

SIR EGLAMOUR *enters.*

EGLAMOUR

> The setting sun begins to color the western sky, and now it's almost the time that Sylvia is supposed to meet me at Friar Patrick's chamber. She will not fail, because those who are in love are always on time, unless they arrive early to speed up their progress.

SYLVIA *enters.*

> See, here she comes now. Good evening, my lady!

SYLVIA

> Thank God, thank God! Go on, my good Eglamour. Go out to the back door by the abbey wall. I'm afraid some spies have followed me.

EGLAMOUR

> Don't worry. The forest is less than nine miles away. If we make it there, we are safe.

They exit.

ACT 5, SCENE 2

Enter THURIO, PROTEUS, *and* JULIA *(disguised in page's attire)*

THURIO
Sir Proteus, what says Sylvia to my suit?

PROTEUS
O, sir, I find her milder than she was,
And yet she takes exceptions at your person.

THURIO
What, that my leg is too long?

PROTEUS
No, that it is too little.

THURIO
I'll wear a boot, to make it somewhat rounder.

JULIA
(*Aside*) But love will not be spurred to what it loathes.

THURIO
What says she to my face?

PROTEUS
She says it is a fair one.

THURIO
Nay, then, the wanton lies; my face is black.

PROTEUS
But pearls are fair, and the old saying is,
Black men are pearls in beauteous ladies' eyes.

JULIA
(*Aside*) 'Tis true, such pearls as put out ladies' eyes,
For I had rather wink than look on them.

THURIO
How likes she my discourse?

PROTEUS
Ill, when you talk of war.

ACT 5, SCENE 2

THURIO, PROTEUS, *and* JULIA *enter.* JULIA *is disguised in the clothing of a male servant.*

THURIO

Sir Proteus, what does Sylvia have to say about my declarations of love for her?

PROTEUS

Oh, sir, she's not as cold as she used to be, though she still objects to you.

THURIO

What, because my leg is too long?

PROTEUS

No, because it's too skinny.

THURIO

I'll wear a boot with spurs, then, to make it look thicker.

JULIA

(*Aside*) But love can't be spurred to like what it hates.

THURIO

What does she have to say about my face?

PROTEUS

She says it is an attractive one.

THURIO

No, then, she's lying—my face is ugly.

PROTEUS

But pearls are beautiful, and the old saying is that ugly men are pearls in beautiful women's eyes.

JULIA

(*Aside*) It's true—the kind of **pearls that make ladies go blind**. I'd rather shut my eyes than look at them.

THURIO

How does she like my conversation?

PROTEUS

Not much, when you talk about war.

Meaning cataracts, a condition in which the lens of the eye grows opaque and white, blurring vision and making the eye somewhat resemble a pearl.

THURIO
But well when I discourse of love and peace?
JULIA
(*Aside*) But better, indeed, when you hold your peace.

THURIO
What says she to my valor?
PROTEUS
O, sir, she makes no doubt of that.
JULIA
(*Aside*) She needs not, when she knows it cowardice.
THURIO
What says she to my birth?
PROTEUS
That you are well derived.
JULIA
(*Aside*) True; from a gentleman to a fool.
THURIO
Considers she my possessions?
PROTEUS
O, ay, and pities them.
THURIO
Wherefore?
JULIA
(*Aside*) That such an ass should owe them.
PROTEUS
That they are out by lease.

Enter DUKE

JULIA
Here comes the Duke.
DUKE
How now, Sir Proteus? how now, Thurio?
Which of you saw Sir Eglamour of late?
THURIO
Not I.

THURIO
> But she likes it when I talk about love and peace?

JULIA
> (*Aside*) But even better when you hold your peace and don't talk at all.

THURIO
> What does she have to say about my bravery?

PROTEUS
> Oh, sir, she doesn't question it at all.

JULIA
> (*Aside*) She doesn't need to, since she knows he's a coward.

THURIO
> What does she have to say about my lineage?

PROTEUS
> That you are of good descent.

JULIA
> (*Aside*) True—he's descended from a gentleman to a fool.

THURIO
> Has she thought about all the lands that I own?

PROTEUS
> Oh, yes, and she pities them.

THURIO
> Why?

JULIA
> (*Aside*) Because an ass like him owns them.

PROTEUS
> Because you've leased them to others.

The DUKE *enters.*

JULIA
> Here comes the Duke.

DUKE
> How are you, Sir Proteus? How are you, Thurio? Have either of you seen Eglamour lately?

THURIO
> I haven't.

PROTEUS
　　　　　　Nor I.
DUKE
　　　　　　　　Saw you my daughter?
PROTEUS
　　　　　　　　　　　　Neither.
DUKE
Why then, she's fled unto that peasant Valentine,
And Eglamour is in her company.
'Tis true, for Friar Lawrence met them both
As he in penance wandered through the forest.
Him he knew well, and guessed that it was she,
But, being masked, he was not sure of it.
Besides, she did intend confession
At Patrick's cell this even, and there she was not.
These likelihoods confirm her flight from hence.
Therefore, I pray you, stand not to discourse,
But mount you presently, and meet with me
Upon the rising of the mountain foot
That leads toward Mantua, whither they are fled.
Dispatch, sweet gentlemen, and follow me.

Exit DUKE

THURIO
Why, this it is to be a peevish girl,
That flies her fortune when it follows her.
I'll after, more to be revenged on Eglamour
Than for the love of reckless Sylvia.

Exit THURIO

PROTEUS
And I will follow, more for Sylvia's love
Than hate of Eglamour that goes with her.

Exit PROTEUS

JULIA
And I will follow, more to cross that love
Than hate for Sylvia, that is gone for love.

Exit

PROTEUS

Nor have I.

DUKE

Have you seen my daughter?

PROTEUS

I haven't seen her either.

DUKE

That means she's run off to that rascal Valentine, and Eglamour is with her. I know it's true, because Friar Lawrence met them both as he wandered through the forest in penance. He knew Eglamour well and guessed that the girl was Sylvia, but he wasn't sure since she had a mask on. Besides, she'd planned to take confession at Friar Patrick's chamber tonight, but she didn't show up. These coincidences confirm that she's run away. Therefore, I beg you, stop talking and mount your horses immediately. Meet me on the rise at the foot of the mountain that leads toward Mantua, where they fled to. Hurry, kind gentlemen, and follow me.

The DUKE *exits.*

THURIO

Why, what a silly girl she is to throw away everything good that was coming to her. I'll follow them, more to get revenge on Eglamour than out of love for reckless Sylvia.

THURIO *exits.*

PROTEUS

And I'll follow, too, more out of love for Sylvia than hatred of Eglamour, who goes with her.

PROTEUS *exits.*

JULIA

And I will follow as well, more to thwart Proteus's love for Sylvia than out of any hatred of Sylvia, who flees because of love.

Exit.

ACT 5, SCENE 3

Enter SYLVIA, OUTLAWS

FIRST OUTLAW
    Come, come,
    Be patient. We must bring you to our captain.

SYLVIA
    A thousand more mischances than this one
    Have learned me how to brook this patiently.

SECOND OUTLAW
5   Come, bring her away.

FIRST OUTLAW
    Where is the gentleman that was with her?

SECOND OUTLAW
    Being nimble-footed, he hath outrun us,
    But Moses and Valerius follow him.
    Go thou with her to the west end of the wood;
10   There is our captain. We'll follow him that's fled.
    The thicket is beset; he cannot scape.
                  Exeunt all but FIRST OUTLAW *and* SYLVIA

FIRST OUTLAW
    Come, I must bring you to our captain's cave.
    Fear not; he bears an honorable mind
    And will not use a woman lawlessly.

SYLVIA
15   O Valentine, this I endure for thee!

                                      Exeunt

ACT 5, SCENE 3

SYLVIA *enters, led by* OUTLAWS.

FIRST OUTLAW
Come on, come on. Be patient. We must bring you to our captain.

SYLVIA
A thousand misfortunes worse than this one have taught me how to endure this patiently.

SECOND OUTLAW
Go on, take her away.

FIRST OUTLAW
Where is **the gentleman that was with her**?

Meaning Eglamour.

SECOND OUTLAW
He was fast so he outran us, but Moses and Valerius are following him. Go with her to the west end of the woods. Our captain is there. We'll follow the guy who fled. The woods are surrounded by our men—he cannot escape.

They all exit, except the FIRST OUTLAW *and* SYLVIA.

FIRST OUTLAW
Come on, I must take you to our captain's cave. Don't be afraid. He is an honorable man and will not rape you.

SYLVIA
Oh, Valentine, I endure all this for you!

They exit.

ACT 5, SCENE 4

Enter VALENTINE

VALENTINE
How use doth breed a habit in a man!
This shadowy desert, unfrequented woods,
I better brook than flourishing peopled towns.
Here can I sit alone, unseen of any,
And to the nightingale's complaining notes
Tune my distresses and record my woes.
O thou that dost inhabit in my breast,
Leave not the mansion so long tenantless,
Lest, growing ruinous, the building fall
And leave no memory of what it was!
Repair me with thy presence, Sylvia;
Thou gentle nymph, cherish thy forlorn swain!
(Shouting within.)
What halloing and what stir is this to-day?
These are my mates, that make their wills their law,
Have some unhappy passenger in chase.
They love me well, yet I have much to do
To keep them from uncivil outrages.
Withdraw thee, Valentine. Who's this comes here?
(He stands aside.)

Enter PROTEUS, SYLVIA, *and* JULIA *(disguised as Sebastian)*

PROTEUS
Madam, this service I have done for you—
Though you respect not aught your servant doth—
To hazard life and rescue you from him
That would have forced your honor and your love.
Vouchsafe me, for my meed, but one fair look;
A smaller boon than this I cannot beg,
And less than this, I am sure, you cannot give.

ACT 5, SCENE 4

NO FEAR SHAKESPEARE

ACT 5, SCENE 4

VALENTINE *enters.*

VALENTINE

Repetition can become habit in a man! This shadowy deserted place, these woods that are rarely visited—I can take them better than bustling towns with lots of people. Here I can sit alone without anyone seeing me, and accompanied by the nightingale's sad song I can sing about my worries and list all my troubles. Oh you, Sylvia, who lives in my heart, don't leave this home empty for long, or rotting from within, the entire building falls and leaves no trace of what it was! Heal me with your presence, Sylvia. Gentle nymph, cherish your sad lover!

(Shouting is heard inside.)

What's all this shouting and commotion I hear? Those are my friends, the outlaws who do whatever they like, who are chasing some unfortunate traveler. They like me enough, but I have to work hard to keep them from violent crimes. Hide yourself, Valentine. Who is this that comes here?

(He stands off to the side.)

PROTEUS, **SYLVIA**, *and* **JULIA**, *who is disguised as Sebastian, enter.*

PROTEUS

Madame, I've helped you—even though you don't value what I do—and risked my life to rescue you from that man who would have raped you. For my reward, give me just one kind look. I can't beg for a smaller favor than this, and I'm sure that you can't give anything less than this.

VALENTINE
    (*Aside*) How like a dream is this I see and hear!
    Love, lend me patience to forbear awhile.

SYLVIA
    O miserable, unhappy that I am!

PROTEUS
    Unhappy were you, madam, ere I came;
30   But by my coming I have made you happy.

SYLVIA
    By thy approach thou mak'st me most unhappy.

JULIA
    (*Aside*) And me, when he approacheth to your presence.

SYLVIA
    Had I been seizèd by a hungry lion,
    I would have been a breakfast to the beast
35   Rather than have false Proteus rescue me.
    O! heaven be judge how I love Valentine,
    Whose life's as tender to me as my soul!
    And full as much—for more there cannot be—
    I do detest false, perjured Proteus.
40   Therefore begone, solicit me no more.

PROTEUS
    What dangerous action, stood it next to death,
    Would I not undergo for one calm look?
    O, 'tis the curse in love, and still approved,
    When women cannot love where they're beloved!

SYLVIA
45   When Proteus cannot love where he's beloved.
    Read over Julia's heart, thy first, best love,
    For whose dear sake thou didst then rend thy faith
    Into a thousand oaths, and all those oaths
    Descended into perjury, to love me.
50   Thou hast no faith left now, unless thou'dst two,
    And that's far worse than none. Better have none
    Than plural faith, which is too much by one.
    Thou counterfeit to thy true friend!

NO FEAR SHAKESPEARE

VALENTINE

(*Aside*) What I see and hear is like a dream! Love, give me strength to be patient just a little while longer.

SYLVIA

Oh, what a miserable, unhappy woman I am!

PROTEUS

You were unhappy, madame, before I came. But in coming I've made you happy.

SYLVIA

Your advances make me very unhappy.

JULIA

(*Aside*) And make me unhappy when he flirts with you.

SYLVIA

If a hungry lion had seized me, I would rather have been eaten by the beast than have treacherous Proteus rescue me. Oh, heaven knows how I love Valentine, whose life is as precious to me as my own soul! And with just as much feeling—for I couldn't feel any more strongly—I hate the lying, deceitful Proteus. So get out of here, and stop trying to win me.

PROTEUS

What dangerous action, even if it put me at risk of death, would I not undertake for just one gentle look from you? Oh, it is the curse of love, and it is always the case that women never love those who love them!

SYLVIA

You mean Proteus never loves those who love him. Think of Julia's feelings for you. She was your first, best love, and for her sake you swore your fidelity a thousand times. Now those oaths of faithfulness have sunk into lies, so that you can love me. You have no loyalty left now, unless you were to love two women, and that's far worse than loving no one. Better not love at all than love two women, which is too many by one. You deceiver of your true friend!

PROTEUS
In love,
Who respects friend?

SYLVIA
All men but Proteus.

PROTEUS
Nay, if the gentle spirit of moving words
Can no way change you to a milder form,
I'll woo you like a soldier, at arms' end,
And love you 'gainst the nature of love—force ye.

SYLVIA
O heaven!

PROTEUS
(*Assailing her*) I'll force thee yield to my desire.

VALENTINE
(*Coming forward*) Ruffian, let go that rude uncivil touch,
Thou friend of an ill fashion!

PROTEUS
Valentine!

VALENTINE
Thou common friend, that's without faith or love!
For such is a friend now. Treacherous man,
Thou hast beguiled my hopes. Naught but mine eye
Could have persuaded me. Now I dare not say
I have one friend alive; thou wouldst disprove me.
Who should be trusted, when one's right hand
Is perjured to the bosom? Proteus,
I am sorry I must never trust thee more,
But count the world a stranger for thy sake.
The private wound is deepest. O time most accurst,
'Mongst all foes that a friend should be the worst!

PROTEUS
My shame and guilt confounds me.
Forgive me, Valentine. If hearty sorrow

ACT 5, SCENE 4
NO FEAR SHAKESPEARE

PROTEUS

Who honors their friendships when it comes to love?

SYLVIA

All men but you, Proteus.

PROTEUS

No, if the gentle spirit of heartfelt words can't persuade you to think kindly of me, then I'll woo you at knifepoint like a soldier and make love to you in a manner contrary to the nature of love—by raping you.

SYLVIA

Oh, heaven!

(PROTEUS assaults her.)

PROTEUS

I'll force you to yield to my desire.

(VALENTINE comes out of hiding.)

VALENTINE

Scoundrel, keep your savage hands off her, you foul friend!

PROTEUS

Valentine!

VALENTINE

You lying friend, without loyalty or love! That's what you are now. Treacherous man, you tricked me with my hopes. Nothing could have persuaded me of what you really are but seeing it with my eyes. Now I won't even say I have one friend alive—if I did, you'd prove me wrong. Who can you trust when your closest friend is false down to his core? Proteus, I'm sorry I must never trust you again, and because of you I'll never think again that I know the world. Personal treachery makes the deepest wound. Curse the day when a friend is the worst of all your enemies!

PROTEUS

Shame and guilt overwhelm me. Forgive me, Valentine. If heartfelt sadness is enough punishment for what I've

Two Gentlemen of Verona   Act 5, Scene 4

> Be a sufficient ransom for offence,
> I tender't here. I do as truly suffer
> As e'er I did commit.

VALENTINE
> Then I am paid,
> And once again I do receive thee honest.
> Who by repentance is not satisfied
> Is nor of heaven nor earth, for these are pleased.
> By penitence the Eternal's wrath's appeased;
> And, that my love may appear plain and free,
> All that was mine in Sylvia I give thee.

JULIA
> O me unhappy!
>
> *(Swoons)*

PROTEUS
> Look to the boy.

VALENTINE
> Why, boy!
> Why, wag! How now? What's the matter? Look up.
> Speak.

JULIA
> (*Recovering*) O good sir, my master charged me to deliver
> a ring to Madam Sylvia, which, out of my neglect, was
> never done.

PROTEUS
> Where is that ring, boy?

JULIA
> (*Giving her own ring*) Here 'tis. This is it.

PROTEUS
> How? Let me see.
> Why, this is the ring I gave to Julia.

JULIA
> O, cry you mercy, sir, I have mistook.
> This is the ring you sent to Sylvia.
>
> *(She offers another ring.)*

ACT 5, SCENE 4
NO FEAR SHAKESPEARE

done, then I offer it to you here. I feel truly miserable for everything I've done.

VALENTINE

Then you've paid your debt to me, and I consider you to be honest once again. Whoever isn't satisfied by such heartfelt repentance is neither from heaven nor earth, for repentance is enough to please both. God's wrath comes in the form of penitence. And, so that you know my love for you is honest and free, I give you any claim I had to Sylvia.

JULIA

Oh, unhappy me!

(She faints.)

PROTEUS

Look at the boy!

VALENTINE

Hey, boy! Hey, kid! Are you okay? What's the matter? Open your eyes. Say something.

JULIA

(*Recovering*) Oh, good sir, my master ordered me to deliver a ring to Madame Sylvia, which, out of neglect on my part, I never did.

PROTEUS

Where is that ring, boy?

JULIA

(*Giving her own ring*) Here it is. This is it.

PROTEUS

How? Let me see that. Why, this is the ring I gave to Julia.

JULIA

Oh, please forgive me, sir, I've made a mistake. This is the ring you sent to Sylvia.

(She hands him another ring.)

PROTEUS
>But how camest thou by this ring?
>At my depart I gave this unto Julia.

JULIA
>And Julia herself did give it me;
>And Julia herself have brought it hither.
>>*(She reveals her identity.)*

PROTEUS
>How? Julia?

JULIA
>Behold her that gave aim to all thy oaths
>And entertained 'em deeply in her heart.
>How oft hast thou with perjury cleft the root!
>O Proteus, let this habit make thee blush!
>Be thou ashamed that I have took upon me
>Such an immodest raiment, if shame live
>In a disguise of love.
>It is the lesser blot, modesty finds,
>Women to change their shapes than men their minds.

PROTEUS
>Than men their minds! 'Tis true. O heaven! Were man
>But constant, he were perfect. That one error
>Fills him with faults, makes him run through all th' sins;
>Inconstancy falls off ere it begins.
>What is in Sylvia's face but I may spy
>More fresh in Julia's with a constant eye?

VALENTINE
>Come, come, a hand from either.
>Let me be blest to make this happy close;
>'Twere pity two such friends should be long foes.
>>*(PROTEUS and JULIA join hands.)*

PROTEUS
>Bear witness, heaven, I have my wish forever.

JULIA
>And I mine.
>*Enter* DUKE *and* THURIO, *led by* OUTLAWS.

ACT 5, SCENE 4

NO FEAR SHAKESPEARE

PROTEUS

But how did you get this ring? I gave it to Julia when I departed from Verona.

JULIA

And Julia herself gave it to me. And Julia herself has brought it here.

(She reveals her identity.)

PROTEUS

What? Julia?

JULIA

It's me, the woman who was the object of all your oaths and believed them deeply in her heart. Your lies have often cut me to the core! Oh, Proteus, I hope my appearance makes you blush! You should be ashamed that I have put on such an immodest outfit, if shame can live in someone who fakes love. Modesty says it's better for women to transform their appearances than for men to change their minds.

PROTEUS

Than for men to change their minds! It's true. Oh, God! Were man more constant and less fickle, he would be perfect. That one error leads to numerous faults and makes him commit all the deadly sins. The fickle man begins deceiving before he even tries to be constant. What does Sylvia have that I wouldn't see to be even better in Julia if I were faithful?

VALENTINE

Come, come on, each of you give me a hand. Let me be blessed to bring this to a happy end. It would be a pity if two such good friends as you were enemies forever.

*(**PROTEUS** and **JULIA** join hands.)*

PROTEUS

As God is my witness, I have what I want forever.

JULIA

And I as well.

*The **DUKE** and **THURIO** enter, led by **OUTLAWS**.*

OUTLAWS
A prize, a prize, a prize!

VALENTINE
Forbear, forbear, I say! it is my lord the Duke.
(The DUKE and THURIO are released.)
Your Grace is welcome to a man disgraced,
Banishèd Valentine.

DUKE
Sir Valentine!

THURIO
(*Advancing*) Yonder is Sylvia, and Sylvia's mine.

VALENTINE
(*Drawing his sword*) Thurio, give back, or else embrace
thy death.
Come not within the measure of my wrath.
Do not name Sylvia thine; if once again,
Verona shall not hold thee. Here she stands.
Take but possession of her with a touch;
I dare thee but to breathe upon my love.

THURIO
Sir Valentine, I care not for her, I.
I hold him but a fool that will endanger
His body for a girl that loves him not.
I claim her not, and therefore she is thine.

DUKE
The more degenerate and base art thou,
To make such means for her as thou hast done
And leave her on such slight conditions.
Now, by the honor of my ancestry,
I do applaud thy spirit, Valentine,
And think thee worthy of an empress' love.
Know then, I here forget all former griefs,
Cancel all grudge, repeal thee home again,
Plead a new state in thy unrivalled merit,
To which I thus subscribe: Sir Valentine,
Thou art a gentleman, and well derived.
Take thou thy Sylvia, for thou hast deserved her.

ACT 5, SCENE 4
NO FEAR SHAKESPEARE

OUTLAWS
> A prize! A prize! A prize!

VALENTINE
> Stop, stop, I say! This is my lord, the duke.
> *(They release the DUKE and THURIO.)*
> I welcome you, Your Grace, as a disgraced man, banished Valentine.

DUKE
> Sir Valentine!

THURIO
> (*Advancing*) Sylvia is over there, and she's mine.

VALENTINE
> (*Drawing his sword*) Thurio, move back, or else be prepared to die. Don't come within a step of my anger. Do not call Sylvia yours. If you do it again, you'll never be welcome in Verona. Go ahead, try to even touch her. I dare you to even breathe upon my love.

THURIO
> Sir Valentine, I don't care about her. I consider anyone a fool who will endanger his life for a girl who doesn't love him. I don't claim her, and therefore she is yours.

DUKE
> Then you are even more degenerate and awful, having made such great efforts to win her as you have and now leaving her for such minor reasons. Now, by the honor of my ancestors, I applaud your spirit, Valentine, and think you worthy of an empress's love. I disregard all my former grievances with you, cancel all grudges, welcome you home again, and give you a clean record because of your unrivaled excellence, which I bear witness to. Sir Valentine, you are a gentleman and wellborn. Take your Sylvia, for you have earned her.

VALENTINE
    I thank Your Grace. The gift hath made me happy.
    I now beseech you, for your daughter's sake,
    To grant one boon that I shall ask of you.

DUKE
    I grant it for thine own, whate'er it be.

VALENTINE
    These banished men, that I have kept withal,
    Are men endued with worthy qualities.
    Forgive them what they have committed here,
    And let them be recalled from their exile.
    They are reformèd, civil, full of good,
    And fit for great employment, worthy lord.

DUKE
    Thou hast prevailed; I pardon them and thee.
    Dispose of them as thou know'st their deserts.
    Come, let us go. We will include all jars
    With triumphs, mirth, and rare solemnity.

VALENTINE
    And, as we walk along, I dare be bold
    With our discourse to make Your Grace to smile.
    What think you of this page, my lord?

DUKE
    I think the boy hath grace in him. He blushes.

VALENTINE
    I warrant you, my lord, more grace than boy.

DUKE
    What mean you by that saying?

VALENTINE
    Please you, I'll tell you as we pass along,
    That you will wonder what hath fortunèd.—
    Come, Proteus, 'tis your penance but to hear
    The story of your loves discoverèd.
    That done, our day of marriage shall be yours:
    One feast, one house, one mutual happiness.

Exeunt

ACT 5, SCENE 4

NO FEAR SHAKESPEARE

VALENTINE

I thank Your Grace. Your gift has made me happy. Now I beg you, for your daughter's sake, to grant one favor that I'll ask of you.

DUKE

I grant it for your own sake, whatever it may be.

VALENTINE

These banished men, whom I have lived with, are men with good qualities. Forgive the crimes they've committed here, and declare an end to their exile. They are reformed, peaceful, good-hearted, and fit for great work, worthy lord.

DUKE

You win. I pardon them and you. I'll leave you in charge of them, since you know what they deserve. Come, let's go. We'll put all quarrels behind us with pageants, happiness, and festivities.

VALENTINE

And, as we walk along, I'd like to be so bold as to tell you something to make Your Grace smile. What do you think of this young servant boy, my lord?

DUKE

I think the boy has a feminine charm. Look, he's blushing.

VALENTINE

I tell you, my lord, there's more feminine charm in him than boy.

DUKE

What do you mean by that?

VALENTINE

If it please you, I'll tell you on the way, and you'll be amazed at what's been going on. Come, Proteus, it's your punishment to hear the story of your two loves revealed. When that's done, our wedding day will also be yours: one feast, one house, and one mutual happiness.

They exit.

Notes